BACKLASH II

More Tales Told by Hunters, Fishermen
and Other Damned Liars

by

Galen Winter

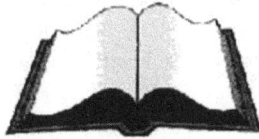

CCB Publishing
British Columbia, Canada

Backlash II: More Tales Told by Hunters, Fishermen and Other
Damned Liars

Copyright ©2010 by Galen Winter
ISBN-13   978-1-926918-10-5
Second Edition

Library and Archives Canada Cataloguing in Publication

Winter, Galen, 1926-
Backlash II : more tales told by hunters, fishermen and other damned liars /
written by Galen Winter – 2nd ed.
These stories have appeared in the Wisconsin sportsman,
The Wisconsin outdoor journal, and Ducks Unlimited magazines.
ISBN 978-1-926918-10-5
I. Title.
PS3573.I53675B332 2010   813'.54   C2010-905957-3

The stories contained herein were first published in *The Wisconsin
Sportsman, The Wisconsin Outdoor Journal* and *Ducks Unlimited*
magazines.

Publisher: CCB Publishing
              British Columbia, Canada
              www.ccbpublishing.com

Contents

Principles

This is the second collection of Backlash columns and articles appearing in *The Wisconsin Sportsman*, *The Wisconsin Outdoor Journal* and the *Ducks Unlimited* magazines.

I wanted to call the first collection: "The King James Version of the Holy Bible." I thought it was a catchy title that might help its sales. I had to give it up when I was informed the title had already been taken.

The Editor, against the advice of his staff and his Board of Directors, decided to publish that first book, but insisted I give it the title: "BACKLASH." He further insisted on its subtitle: "A Compendium of Lore and Lies – Mostly Lies – Concerning Hunting, Fishing and the Out-of-Doors."

Though I harbored serious but unspoken misgivings, I swallowed my pride and agreed. Now another Editor, obviously cut from the same cloth, insists I call this book: "Backlash II - Tales Told by Hunters, Fishermen and Other Damned Liars." This time I must register my objection.

The perceptive reader who carefully studies that proposed title might very easily conclude it leaves the subtle impression that out-of-doors types cannot always be believed. Even such a gentle hint of an accusation that hunters and fishermen might unwittingly tell a fib is an anathema to me. I will not stand for it.

In these days when television ads, politicians' speeches, lawyers' summations to juries and used car salesmen are all given the presumption of truthfulness, to suggest a fisherman is lying when he describes the size of the Arctic Char he caught in one of the tributaries of Brazil's Amazon River staggers the imagination.

The judicial system has fallen into a disgraceful state. Upper Michigan judges will not allow fishermen to testify in open court, even when placed under oath. What is this world coming to?

Surely, anyone who is an active participant in hunting and fishing activities has been acquainted with a sportsman who may have been suspected of occasionally telling the truth. Does the general public know it? Unfortunately, they do not. It is time for us to expose the vile canard that has for so long convinced otherwise rational people to believe out-of-doors types treat the truth with Cavalier distain.

Clearly, a scientific study was needed and I undertook the job. I polled all of my friends - the people who hunt and fish with me. The poll questions were:

1. Are hunters and fishermen paragons of virtue who always, always tell the truth?

- or -

2. Do hunters and fishermen (due to faulty memories or illness) at times (inadvertently and without intent to deceive) occasionally report misstatements of fact?

- or -

3. Other

The results of that poll are instructive. All four votes were cast for Question #1. Since the accuracy of polls is unquestioned, the matter of sportsmen's honesty is, finally, set to rest. We are, all of us, honest and marvelous citizens.

I hurried to the Editor's office, threw the poll documents on his desk and triumphantly exclaimed: "See, smarty pants!" I watched his lips move as he read the poll results. You can imagine my consternation when, nevertheless, he still insisted on his proposed title.

It now became a matter of principle. Should I again accede to the Philistine demands and, puppy-like, accept an odious title to my work of art simply because I wanted to get the book published and make a lot of royalty money? Should I genuflect to commercial interest or should I maintain my independence and refuse to allow my work to be prostituted?

I told the Editor he could take his title and stick it. I told him I didn't give a damn if he refused to publish my opus. I told him I would stand on my principles, come hell or high water, and I stormed out of his office. That was the end of it. Let it be a lesson to you. Always be guided by your principles.

Galen Winter
Shawano, WI

(NOTE: You have just been conned into reading the Author's Preface.)

Post Mortem Fishing

A number of older fishermen and a few younger ones who have been playing around with married women have foreseen the possibility of death staring them straight in the face. As a result they have become more than casually interested in learning if there is any fishing in the after life and, if so, where can they get tips to help them prepare for an eternity of post mortem fishing.

It has been suggested that I investigate the matter and inform the interested parties of the results. Credible source material was not easy to obtain. Religious leaders and the Department of Natural Resource folks were contacted and engaged in serious discussion. The ministers, rabbis, priests and mullahs didn't venture an opinion. They told me I should go to Heaven if I wanted accurate information. The DNR folks also passed the buck. When I called them, they told me to go to hell and hung up. I followed the advice of both parties and am now able to give you this authoritative report.

Yes, in Heaven excellent fishing is available. If fly fishing is your predilection, in the Trout Fishing Section of New Jerusalem it is always June. The streams running through it contain substantial populations of German Brown trout as big as your leg. There is an unbroken Grey Drake hatch. The Elysian Fields produce a bumper crop of grasshoppers. Dave's Hopper is the recommended terrestrial (or should I say "celestial") artificial fly.

The lakes up there are the homes for humongous Muskies.

The minimum size limit is 55 inches and a review of heavenly records shows not a single instance of a smaller Musky being hooked or even seen followed a plug. Though known as the "fish of a thousand casts" here on earth, up there the Musky is commonly called "the fish of ten casts".

Walleyes, as well as large Perch and other pan fish abound in the Heavenly lakes. Huge Big Mouth Bass are vicious in their attacks of artificial lures. Because fish dinners are provided free of charge in Valhalla, all fishing is Catch and Release, thereby releasing the fisherman of the onerous job of convincing his wife to scale and clean the fish.

The seasons of the year are divided according to interest and usage instead of chronologically. If you prefer to ice fish, the Winter Sport Season of Paradise has lakes frozen over three hundred and sixty five days a year (366 during leap years). Special frozen lakes and rivers are reserved for Sturgeon spearing. Ice shanties and spearing blinds need never be removed from the lakes since there is no spring thaw in that part of Heaven.

In the Summer Lake Fishing Section of Heaven, all outboard motors are required to start on the first crank. They use neither oil nor gasoline and deep cell batteries for trolling motors never have to be recharged. Lakes and streams are not crowded, rod tips are never broken and there is no DNR. That's why they call it "Paradise".

As a special favor, St. Peter reviewed admission records back to the time the Place was established. Except for the Saints who netted fish in the Sea of Galilee before getting religion and giving up the sport, no fisherman has ever been admitted to Heaven. Fishermen were and continue to be such terrible liars that not one of them has ever come close to meeting the heavenly SAT exam requirements. This accounts for the fact the lakes and streams are never crowded.

Having never been known to treat the truth with anything but the highest degree of respect, I fully expect to be allowed to enter the Elysian Fields. I look forward to fishing in Paradise (but not in the immediate future). You, on the other hand, should preserve no such hope or expectation since the potential of your going to Heaven is limited to the point of being non-existent. However, an alternative is open to you. Since you cannot possibly go to Heaven, I refer, of course, to the potential of your enjoyment of fishing in Hell.

Though not a fisherman himself, Satan has not overlooked the establishment of special facilities for those of his guests who engaged in the sport while on earth. After all, many of his resident clientele are fishermen. (The largest local population is made up of women. Recently an Affirmative Action Regulation has been adopted and in the future no more men will be admitted until a one-to-one woman to man ratio is attained.)

Charon, the boatman who ferries the condemned souls over the River Styx and up to the gates of Hades, operates a fly shop and a guide service on that river. Due to the large number of fishermen, used car salesmen, politicians and attorneys dying and being sent to Hell, the poor fellow spends most of his days operating his ferry. The time available for river guiding is quite limited.

(For the information of all of you hunters, Cerberus, Hell's three headed dog guarding the entrance to Hades, is an excellent bird hunter. When the dog is not engaged in ripping the stuffing out of the new arrivals, Charon will rent him out. The animal loves to hunt upland birds and has been known to point three Hungarian Partridge at the same time.)

At the Gates of Hell, the River Styx is too warm to support trout of any sort. Small Mouth Bass and pan fish are about all that can be caught on that part of the river. Trout fishermen are advised to travel a few miles up stream where a water temperature of 60 degrees is maintained throughout the year. Brooks, Browns and Rainbow are all present in both large numbers and sizes.

The trout are attracted by only a few artificial flies. They are the Hellgrammite, Black Prince, Gray Ghost and Golden Demon. Lake fish, of course, prefer the old fashioned Daredevil.

Hell is graced by a large number of officials from the various Departments of Natural Recourses. This accounts for the multitude of intricate, conflicting and incomprehensible regulations which govern stream, lake and fish management. In spite of their presence, the Hellish fisheries have always and will continue to contain record sized trophies.

Before preparing for your trip to Hades, you should be aware of the fact that down there the hunting and fishing seasons are perpetually closed. That's why they call it Hell.

Trivial Pursuit

There was a terrible fuss over at the Hillman's last Saturday night. It all started when Jerry and Joy invited What's-Her-Name and me to their house for a six pack of milk and a hand of Trivial Pursuit. Whoever created that game hates civilization and is out to destroy us all.

First of all, I've never been able to develop great enthusiasm for any game that isn't played with two or five dice. Those which require only one die are not natural. How can you roll a seven? Just try playing Liar's Dice with only one cube. It'll shorten the game and take all the fun out of it.

The world would be better off if there were no "one die" games and if Congress really had our better interest at heart, they'd stop posturing and making meaningless, self-serving speeches and pass a law to suppress all one die games.

Second, I lose patience with games that cheat. A little sleight of hand by the participants at the poker table is to be expected and adds spice to what otherwise might be a dull evening at deer camp - although it sometimes results in gun shot wounds. All other games should be honest.

In Trivial Pursuit, if your answer isn't right, you lose. I've got no problem with that general thesis - but the damned game lies. It's worse than a waste of time. The game of Trivial Pursuit should be outlawed - if only for the children's sake. Society has an obligation to educate them and it can't be done if people insist on feeding them a lot of false information through that ridiculous game.

Now friends, if you are skeptical, just listen to what happened to me last Saturday. Everything started out nice and friendly and Joy explained the game. As I understand it, you shake the one die, move a marker in one direction or another and then the person to your right asks a question. Simple enough, right?

I positioned myself to Jerry's right and after he shook, I asked him: "Just where were you last fall when you ran into all those coveys of Ruffed Grouse?" He told me it was none of my business and I got a little disgusted with him right then and there. It didn't seem to me like he was playing the game.

Then I think Joy changed the rules. She told me I couldn't ask the questions. The game did the asking and the questions came printed on a little card. The one Jerry got was: "Name the starting line-up of the 1922 Chicago Black Sox." Jerry could only remember eight, so he lost.

It was What's-Her-Name's turn next and I didn't particularly like her answer to the question: "What is the most intelligent sub-human primate?" I suppose she meant it as a compliment, but I gave her a dirty look anyway.

This business about the game asking the questions wouldn't be so bad if the questions made any sense, but it doesn't take much time to figure out the fellow who prepared the questions had a diseased mind. Who but a person suffering from serious psychic disorders would write a question for the Sports Category as follows: "How many hoops are there in an Association Croquet Court?"

I don't want to offend all of you croquet shooters. (I had a cousin who used to do it. He was a strange cousin.) Still, I really don't consider croquet to be a sport and I think it amounts to out and out fraud to put that question in the Sports Category.

This whole concept of letting the game ask all the questions casts serious doubt on its basic fairness. Not only that. Some of those questions would tax the memory and knowledge of Mr. Britannica or whoever it was who wrote the encyclopedia. For instance, how many nails are in a standard horseshoe? (Who cares?) What does the Kelvin scale measure? (Kelvinators?) What does a Piscatologist excel in?

I took a guess at that one, missed it by a mile and got back that dirty look I had already given to What's-Her-Name. It turns out that a Piscatologist is a fisherman. If I were you, I'd be careful who I called a Piscatologist - especially if he is bigger than you.

These criticisms aside, the most objectionable feature of Trivial Pursuit is: the game answers its own questions. Moreover, the answer on the card is the only one that counts. There is no room for any argument, no partial score for being part right and no right of appeal to a higher authority - no matter how wrong that card's answer is. This is not only unfair. It's un-American. We fought a war to do away with Hitler and now this game wants to impose the same type of autocratic control over our lives.

Here are some examples: Question - "Who ran off with a pussy cat?" Answer: "The Owl, in a beautiful pea green boat." The hell it was an owl. It was Alex Schubert and there's no question about it, he ran off with a real pussy cat. Incidentally, it wasn't a "beautiful pea green boat", either. It was a restored blue 1976 Corvette - but Trivial Pursuit insists it was an owl and there's no arguing with it.

Here's another one. Question: "What non-mechanical sport achieves the highest speed?" Answer: "Sky Diving". This is absolute nonsense. Whoever made up that answer never saw Ted Johnson, with his fly rod intact and his creel full of speckled trout, being chased across that cleared forty next to Mill Creek by Teetzen's bull.

We had gone around the table three or four times without anyone giving a correct answer. There had been some violent arguments and some of us weren't speaking to others of us. It got to be my turn and the question was: "What important Western Hemisphere event occurred on July Fourth?"

Friends, I had the answer to that one and figured I'd win the game for sure and get a box of shells, a pair of tip-ups, some hand tied flies, or something like that. Well, the three of them got jealous and said the answer was the Declaration of Independence. They all claimed it occurred on that date.

That may be so, but it was also on July 4th that I caught a 26 inch Brown Trout on the Peshtigo River. They said the Declaration of Independence was more important. Imagine! We never got to see the answer on the card because I ripped it up and threw it away.

Relations in the neighborhood stayed strained for a few days and then the three of them got together and finally admitted they were wrong and I was right. We're friendly again, but I don't think we'll play Trivial Pursuit any more.

Metamorphosis

Man has learned to live with The Bomb, Global Warming, Global Cooling, the Black Plague, Acid Rain, Asbestos Insulation, Unruly Wives and liberals. In spite of the threatening presence of those terrible catastrophes, he has learned to cope. He is able to lead a reasonably serene and pleasant existence - but only if his cabin is not occupied by pine squirrels.

Henry Robinson is a case in point. Henry supported all pseudo-environmentalist and Animal Rights organizations. He believed all of the world's problems were directly or indirectly caused by gun ownership and could be solved if every firearm was confiscated and all gun owners were sent to prison for life - without either trial or possibility of parole.

Henry owned a cabin situated deep in the woods of Vilas County. Until the snows and springtime mud made it impossible to negotiate the two rut road leading to it, Henry would spend nearly every weekend in his hideaway, searching for morels, honey mushrooms and other edible fungi, putting out food for the birds and otherwise communing with nature.

In April, as soon as the weather and temperature allowed an artfully driven 4-wheel drive vehicle to successfully fight its way to his cabin, Henry Robinson would leave the city and travel north to open his cabin and prepare for the coming season's beautiful experiences with the flora and fauna of the wild woods. It was one of his rites of spring.

Last year, when he made his first visit to the cabin, he

opened the door, saw the condition of its interior and was aghast. What he saw brought him to a new and more complete understanding of the word "mess". Pots and pans were scattered in the kitchen area. Paper toweling had been shredded. Even the snow shoes decorating his wall had been knocked down and the webbing destroyed.

Upon seeing this and other outrages, at first Henry thought the Dark Age Vikings or the more modern Clockwork Orange gang had appeared and sacked the place. Then he saw a pine squirrel scurry through the hole it had chewed in the ceiling and up into the safety of the attic.

Further investigation showed a second hole, slightly larger than a silver dollar, had been gnawed through the outer wall of the cabin. Henry knew what had happened. After he had closed the cabin in November, driven by the cold, a pine squirrel, one of Mother Nature's woodsy creatures, had entered his building. Mother Nature's woodsy creature chewed the hell out of Henry's mattress in order to get enough material to build its own nest in the attic insulation.

The squirrel, unconcerned with snow or sleet or wind chill temperatures, wintered there in his snug attic sanctuary. From time to time it would rouse from it half-sleep hibernation, descend and chew the hell out of whatever had been left unchewed on the main floor of the cabin. Henry's love and admiration for Mother Nature's woodsy creatures took a backstep.

Many human beings know there are various powders and pastes that will terminally discourage ants, mosquitoes and black gnats. Even wood ticks present no problem to those people because they have the foresight to provide themselves with N-Diethyl- meta-toluamide laden sprays. They know mouse poison will take care of mice. They know rat poison will kill pine squirrels.

For many human beings who don't like to use poison to discourage the uninvited pine squirrels from entering their cabins, there is an obvious solution. Get a gun and shoot the destructive little (deleted). In Henry Robinson's case, the question was: How do you get rid of pine squirrels if you don't like to use poisons and believe guns are nasty?

Henry Robinson was a proud member of all Animal Rights groups. The thought of imposing capital punishment on the offending squirrel never occurred to him. He opened two cans of beans, cleaned the covers and nailed them over the holes in the walls. He went home believing he had humanely evicted his non-rent paying animal guests.

During the week an awful thought occurred to him. By nailing can covers over the holes, he may have trapped the squirrel inside his cabin. Would it be unable to get out? Would the creature die inside the cabin and smell up the place? He bought a wire mesh box trap.

On his next trip north, he was relieved to see new holes drilled next to the ones he had already patched with the tin can covers. He was not relieved to see the hole in the package of flour and the wide distribution of its contents. He was not relieved to see what the pine squirrel had done to his supply of toilet paper.

Remembering squirrels are often seen on bird feeders, Henry concluded they must like seeds. He baited his box trap with the sunflower seeds he stuck into a generous glob of peanut butter. Then he carefully pushed the device into the attic and waited. The next morning the desire result had been obtained. The trap contained a squirrel. The squirrel had a bobbed tail, probably shot off, Henry thought, by some terrible hunter.

As he drove to release the squirrel at a place far distant from his cabin, Henry experienced a shock of recognition. He was surprised to recognize he no longer considered the pine squirrel to be one of his furry friends. He considered it to be a destructive beast that, without provocation, had attacked and vandalized his cabin. He couldn't disguise his sense of elation at having been able to trap it.

Henry turned the squirrel loose in a stand of white pine ten miles away. He returned to his cabin, nailed up more tin can covers and spent a day cleaning the mess in his cabin. On the following weekend, Henry returned to find more holes gnawed through his outer wall and inner ceiling. He also found another mess inside his building. He again set the box trap and again caught the bob tailed squirrel. Again he released it at another distant place and again returned to again clean up the squirrel's mess.

During the following weeks, the catch and release scenario was repeated and it became obvious. The bob-tailed squirrel considered itself to be the owner of the cabin. Henry still tried to get rid of it in what he called a "humane" fashion. He put a plate of candy in the attic, hoping the animal would eat it, develop tooth decay and be unable to chew through his cabin walls. He fed it dog food and called it "Rover" in a desperate attempt to con it into thinking it was a dog and get it to play with Bruno, the neighbor's vicious Pit Bull. Nothing worked.

The pine squirrel stayed in the attic and became more and more gnawingly abusive. Henry had nightmares. He dreamed he was trapped in a surrealistic version of Poe's The Raven. It was a pine squirrel perched above his chamber door. In answer to Henry's demand that it leave his cabin, the animal always answered: "Nevermore."

Henry became more and more agitated. It didn't help when his insurance agent told him his policy covered vandalism only if was occasioned by human beings. Destruction by pine squirrels was considered to be an "Act of God." Henry blew up. He cancelled the insurance and resigned from the church.

Henry Robinson learned to cope and now leads a peaceful and serene life. The letters of resignation he sent to the Animal Rights groups can only be described as containing some very strong language. "Destructive little S--- of a B-----" was one of the milder phrases. Henry is now a member of the National Rifle Association. He owns shotguns, rifles, pistols and revolvers. He is a good shot.

The bob-tailed squirrel has gone to his reward.

Pine squirrels no longer bother Henry's cabin. His property is the black hole of squirreldom. If a pine squirrel has the temerity to venture close to Henry's domain, it is sucked into an explosive vortex and disappears forever. Mother pine squirrels instruct their young to give Henry Robinson's cabin a wide berth.

Spaghetti

It is the common practice of Editors of outdoor sport magazines to insinuate written text between the columns of advertisements which appear in their publications. As the magazines prosper and more and more manufacturers of sports equipment insist upon purchasing advertising space, Editors have become hard pressed to find stories and article to fill those in-between spaces.

Some of them, in desperation, have actually resorted to paying good money for articles dealing with the cooking of game and the preparation of camp foods. A lot of these stories are accompanied by color photographs which show pictures of the finished product.

The perceptive reader will immediately recognize the fraud embodied in most such articles. For instance - in all of those photos, you will note the knives, forks and spoons all have the same pattern. I defy you to find a real hunting camp which contains even a single set of matching knife, fork and spoon.

The pictures also show food which actually appears to be good to eat. Now I don't mean to suggest the food served in all hunting and fishing camps is venomous. It isn't. Not in all camps. The food prepared in, perhaps, seventy percent of them is probably non-toxic.

The other thirty percent, however, represent a clear and present danger to the health and well-being of the out-doorsman. Any reasonably experienced hunter or fisherman knows the local Department of Health will pay a bounty of one hundred dollars in cash for the dead bodies of most camp cooks. If you bring them in alive, they won't pay anything and if you leave them in their office, they'll fine you for littering.

Such being the case, any wise outdoorsman will select his hunting/fishing companions with care, making sure at least one of his associates is kitchen competent. Any truly wise outdoorsman will make sure at least two of his companions are kitchen competent.

Once upon a time, I fished with Carl Wussow and Steve Willett. Both were capable of producing meals on grills, on wood stoves and over camp fires. Often those meals contained vitamins, were tasty and weren't merely poured into a dish from a junk food package or heated directly in the can. I thought two capable cooks would be enough. I was wrong.

We rented a motel room near the shoreline of Montana's Madison River. It had cooking privileges. Since I washed the breakfast dishes, I was exempted from assisting in the preparation of the evening meal. I don't mind doing the breakfast dishes. I have to wash my hands anyway. Besides, we use paper plates and cups. However, as a condition for being relieved of dinner preparation chores, it was given me strictly in charge to make no snide comment, complaint or commentary relative to the cooking process. At the time it seemed fair. I was lucky to be able to live to regret my promise.

Steve and Carl decided to make spaghetti.

For those of you who know nothing about such things, the cooking of spaghetti is an intricate and complicated matter which consists of four separate phases. Step One: Bring water to a boil. Gourmet chefs suggest you bring a pot large enough to hold the water. Another trick is to be sure you turn on the electric stove. With a bit of dry-run instruction followed by practice, most camp cooks can develop the ability to accomplish Step One with reasonable efficiency.

Step Two: Put the spaghetti into the boiling water. Care must be exercised in selecting only hard, uncooked spaghetti. If soft, cooked spaghetti is chucked into the pot, the result will be a terrible sticky mess. I know. I tried it once.

One must be sure to remove those hard sticks of uncooked spaghetti from the plastic bag they come in. If you throw the whole unopened package into the pot, it will all meld together. It will be midnight before you've separated enough strands of the stuff to make a good meal.

Step Three: Take the spaghetti out of the pot. The problem involved in Step Three lies in knowing when to take it out of the pot. The term "al dente" doesn't help much. Bite into it before you add it to the water and you will learn it is very hard and not yet done. Bite into it after it has been cooked an hour or so and you'll learn is very soft and an overdone mess.

The question is: When - between zero and sixty minutes - should you take the spaghetti out of the pot? When is it just right? According to Willett and Wussow, you throw a strand of spaghetti up into the air. If it sticks to the ceiling, it's done.

Step Four: Make the sauce. Some people buy a can of the stuff or a pre-mixed dry concoction which somehow or other gets turned into spaghetti sauce. Other people feel it is essential to add special ingredients to the store-bought product. Beware of these people.

Arthur "Bugs" Baer once said "there is no such thing as a little garlic." He was a wise man. Referring to the spaghetti dinner in question, I am able to tell every one of you - there is such a thing as too much garlic. There is also such a thing as too much crushed red pepper, too much jalapeño and tepin chilies, too much cayenne powder and too much Louisiana Hot Sauce.

Call me timid, pusillanimous and cowardly if you will, but

I don't like my spaghetti to bite into me before I bite into it. Up until the following morning, I believed the term "Ring of Fire" referred to the volcanoes surrounding the rim of the Pacific Ocean. Believe me, friends, as far as I'm concerned and on a very personal level, the term "Ring of Fire" has another meaning.

I no longer like spaghetti. I'm glad I don't like spaghetti because if I did like spaghetti, I'd eat it and if I ate it, I'd run the risk of getting another taste treat like the one I suffered through at that motel on the banks of the Madison River.

Fabulous Fishing

Once upon a time, in a kingdom located on a great trout stream far beyond the Tomorrow River, there lived a king with a real beaut for a daughter. Her name was Rapunzel. The king, remembering how he used to save maidens in distress when he was a young prince, made sure she was well chaperoned when she was outside of the castle. He kept her on a short leash. She spent most of her time in her room on the upper floor of the castle's southwest tower.

Rapunzel knew she was a stunning beauty and she had a pretty high opinion of herself. She enjoyed the appreciative glances of the local lads when they watched her long golden tresses and things bouncing as she walked down the street. She played it real cool and never gave any of them the time of day.

The fellows used to hang around the southwest tower and yell: "Hey, Rapy. Why don't you let your hair down? Yeah, Rapunzel, Rapunzel, let down your long hair." But she'd merely look superior, raise her nose a half inch or so and walk away from the window. Rapunzel had her heart set on espousing Prince Charming.

The Prince was a good looking cuss. He was tall, self assured and had dark curly hair. He wasn't interested in princesses. He hunted and fished and kept dogs. He knew if he married he would spend his weekends doing the chores his bride had dreamed up - like re-chinking the castle or enlarging the moat so it would be bigger than Queen Guenevere's. He knew his hunting and fishing time would be substantially reduced, so he decided princesses were dangerous and he stayed away from them.

Well, one day Charming was walking along a path next to the castle. When Rapunzel saw him, she stuck her head out of the tower window and let her golden hair flow down to the ground. Then she softly and coyly called out "Chaarrming. Chaaaarrrming. You could climb up my long hair and get up here with me if you wanted to." Then she winked at him.

Now Prince Charming was no fool. He wasn't going to get caught by such a transparent trick. Then he thought some other poor fellow might be trapped by Rapunzel's ploy. He wouldn't want that to happen to anyone so he reached inside his tunic, pulled out his fishing knife and cut off eight feet of Rapunzel's golden hair.

That evening the prince went to Ye Olde 400 Bar for a glass or two of mead with his fishing buddies – Porky, the wisest of the Three Little Pigs (he was the one who built his house of brick) and an ugly gnome called Rumpelstilskin. Everyone referred to him as "Rump" because they couldn't remember his real name.

Rump and Porky usually came in after dinner and the three of them would swap fishing stories and discuss the cares of the day and the troubles of the world. The wise little pig, a Technical Advisor working at Uncle Ed's Pork Rind Fishing Lure Company, was the last to arrive. He refused the chicharones the Prince offered him and bought drinks for the house. It was a small "house" - consisting of himself, Prince Charming and Rumpelstilskin. Porky wouldn't have made the offer if Snow White and the seven dwarfs had been there. Like I said, he was a wise little pig.

"Well," said Rump, "you seem pleased with yourself. What are you celebrating?"

"You know the Big Bad Wolf?" Porky answered.

"You mean the one who huffed and puffed and blew down the straw and stick houses of your two brothers?" Rump asked.

"Yeah, that's the one", said Porky. "I just fixed his clock. And I solved another problem at the same time. After he huffed and puffed and destroyed their homes, both brothers moved in with me. They're not nearly as neat as I am. The three of us sharing a one bedroom brick home is not exactly what you might call a wondrous joy. They turned the place into a pig pen.

"And to make matters worse, early every Friday evening, Big Bad comes over and knocks on my door. When I refuse to let him in, he really raises hell. He huffs and he puffs for a while and then goes back to his den. The neighbors are beginning to complain. They call the cops, but by the time they get there, Big Bad is long gone. Those problems are now in the past and I'm celebrating."

Porky looked around to be sure no one else had entered the bar and ordered another round for the house. "Yesterday evening when the knock came," he continued, "I said 'come in' and swung the door open. As soon as Big Bad stuck his head into the room, I beaned him with that 14 inch iron skillet I use to fry smelt. I've got his hide outside in the back of the pick-up. You want to see it?

"Having removed the threat of the wolf as an excuse for staying with me, I gave my brothers their walking papers and they are now on their way down the road."

Porky looked at the Prince and said: "Charmy, you look like the cat that swallowed the canary. That self satisfied smirk must mean you're up to something. I'll bet you've been visiting Cinderella again."

Charming turned a bit pink, but quickly recovered and said: "No, but I sure showed that stuck-up Rapunzel," and he told the boys about cutting off part of her long hair. He gave each of them a handful of the golden locks.

When Rump looked at his watch and said he had to go, Porky and Charming asked why he had to leave so early. The ugly gnome merely looked mysterious and refused to give a direct answer. He said he'd explain everything when they met at the bridge over the Main South Branch of the Oconto for their usual Sunday morning fish.

"And if that bridge Troll gives you any trouble," he said as he left the tavern, "tell him to back off or I'll have aunt Wicked-From-The-West cast a spell on him and turn him into a U. S. Representative and send his to Washington D C. That'll scare the hell out of him".

The next morning, Porky and Prince Charming were waiting at the bridge when Rump drove up. He confessed to stealing Porky's wolf skin and he also confessed to having a second job - trying to teach the king's new wife to spin gold from straw.

"She's not too bright", Rump told his friends. "She can spin very well and her fingers are nimble, but she just can't manage that special knack needed to turn the straw into gold. I made a deal with her last night. I'll spin the gold for her if she'll tie flies and spin fishing line for me. Just take a look at these."

Rump opened a pocket in his fishing vest and took out some #6 weight forward, gold colored fly line and a handful of wonderful Wolf Hair Wing Adams flies. "Take a couple of them," he said. "They look like they might be a perfect match of this morning's hatch. Charmy, do you think you could get some more of Rapunzel's golden hair? I've already got a good supply of wolf hair."

And the three friends went trout fishing and lived happily ever after.

Origins

A million or so years ago, one of our ancestors with opposable thumbs climbed down from a tree. As he wandered out onto a savannah in search of something to eat, he came across a gnawed thighbone of a baboon. He picked it up. Though he couldn't find any meat on it, he thought: "What the hell, maybe it will make good soup." At that very moment, a Saber Toothed tiger came charging at him.

Unable to run back into the forest and scurry up a tree for protection, our ancestor had to stand his ground and fight. He clunked the tiger over the head with the soup bone. This came as a surprise to the tiger. It had been accustomed to being the hunter and not the hunted. The shock was so great it promptly died.

The occurrence also came as a surprise to the humanoid. His search for food seldom led him to Saber Toothed Tiger meat. On the few occasions when he found some, it had been dead for some time and he had to fight off the vultures if he wanted his fair share of it.

This ancient ancestor became the first true hunter. He had discovered both weaponry and a new and exciting way to get non-rancid meat. Many of his clan member friends and companions noticed his constant supply of fresh meat. They became curious. They carefully watched him and discovered his secret. Soon it seemed as if everyone had to have his own thigh bone of a baboon. The shops that sold such things had a difficult time keeping up with the demand.

It wasn't long (geologically speaking) before our pre-historic progenitors were able to come down from the trees and live in more comfortable caves where the results of falling out of bed were less serious. They spent their weekends wandering around the savannahs, far from the safety of climbable trees.

Sooner or later, a hungry Saber Toothed Tiger, thinking it had found an easy meal, would attack. Then the cave man would pull out his baboon thigh bone and clunk the tiger over the head. He'd haul the carcass back to the cave for the little woman to skin and cook.

With more of their number enjoying a nutritious diet of fresh tiger meat and with fewer of their number falling out of trees or otherwise providing Saber Toothed Tigers with a nutritious diet of fresh humanoid meat, the cave men grew bigger and stronger and extended their life expectancy. A major step in the advancement of civilization had taken place - all because of the discovery of weaponry.

More advances allied to the discovery of weapons were forthcoming. In those early days, the wild dogs had a pretty tough time of it. They had no one to scratch their ears. No overstuffed chair to jump into when the cave man was hunting and the cave woman was out looking for nuts and berries. Without toilet bowls, dogs had to get their drinking water from rivers and lakes and puddles.

The wild dog took notice of the large number of Saber Toothed Tiger bones scattered around the entrances of caves and its lifestyle changed forever. The wild dog was no fool. It saw the stack of baboon thigh bones as well as the piles of delicious tiger bones. Preferring not to be clunked over the head, the dogs adopted the policy: "If you can't beat 'em, join 'em." They decided to domesticate.

The erstwhile wild dog became the cave man's best friend. Thus mankind's second great leap forward took place. The hunting dog had evolved. In exchange for retrieving pterodactyls, treeing Saber Toothed Tigers and pointing Hairy Mammoths, the dog got free food and someone to throw sticks for it - advantages still enjoyed by their descendents.

Progress, however, does not come without struggle. Ignorance and superstition are not new. They existed in the cave man's day even though the concept of a Senate and a House of Representatives had not yet been developed.

Then, as now, there were those who militated against change and enlightenment. They had to be dragged, kicking and screaming, into the Stone Age. The inhabitants of a nearby forest, still living in trees, deplored the discovery of the thigh bone club. They claimed the weapon would be used against humanoids as well as tigers and for purposes other than finding food. They were right. When a few of them tried to take weapons from the hunters, they got clunked on the head.

With their thesis thus proven, a group of tree dwellers attempted to create and enforce programs of baboon thigh bone control - you know - thigh bone registration, waiting periods and records checks before purchase, the outlawing of automatic thigh bones and Saturday Night Specials and, in a few cases, the outright banning of all baboon bones.

They had only limited success. Even in the few places where thigh bone control legislation was passed, Humanoids still clunked other humanoids over the head. The old axiom was proven. "Baboon thigh bones don't clunk cave men over the head. Cave men clunk cave men over the head."

With the possible exceptions of the Himalayan Yettis and the... (Is it Big Feet or Big Foots? hmmm.) With the possible exception of the Himalayan Yettis and the creatures represented by those big hairy guys occasionally reported in the Pacific Northwest, there are no descendents of the tree dwelling "thigh bone control faction" of cave man society.

Unable to adjust to reality, like the dinosaurs before them, the thigh-bone-control cave men became extinct.

Other groups of humanoids were convinced the thigh bone weapons were so terrible no clan would dare use them during the raids they undertook for the purpose of kidnapping women from neighboring clans. That group of humanoids was in for a disappointment. Both the raids and the use of the weapons continued. Over the next few decades, all of the males in the clans who bought into the "Too Terrible a Weapon" theory got clunked over the head by their attackers. With the breeding stock thus depleted, they became extinct.

Anthropologists have uncovered evidence of yet another group who opposed the advancement of civilization. This bunch warned that the popularity of the thigh bone weapon would result in the extinction of the baboon. The extinction of one of the earth's creatures, they argued, far outweighed any possible advantage baboon bone weapons could produce. As a matter of principle, they refused to eat meat dragged into camp by the hunters. Those who didn't starve to death became vegetarians.

By this time, the cave man hunters had developed their own lobby group - Baboons Unlimited. BU held annual banquets and raised funds for the preservation of baboon habitat. The debate between the Baboon Thigh Bone people and Anti-Baboon Thigh Bone people continues to this day. One fact is clear: The baboons are not an endangered species.

* * * * *

AUTHOR'S NOTE: Something else is also clear. The Saber Toothed Tiger is extinct. In my opinion, Saber Toothed Tiger extinction shouldn't bother anyone. If there were efforts to reintroduce the Saber Toothed Tiger into the woods, I suspect the practice of deer hunting would become extinct. That would bother me.

Hans

Laconic and taciturn folks are not treated fairly by the rest of the inhabitants of the universe. As soon as someone develops a reputation for being close-mouthed, the chances are that "someone" will also develop the reputation of not being very smart. There's no logic to it. If you keep your mouth shut, no one can prove you're not very bright. It's when you open your mouth that you run the risk of providing the proof.

I hunted ducks with Hans for six or seven seasons and we never really had a conversation. Hans was one of those monosyllabic types. You know - the kind that volunteers no information and limits his participation in discussions to one word responses.

To give you an example, one Saturday in early October, Hans and I were in a duck blind built on the shoreline of Boulder Lake. On the previous day, I completed some necessary work on my cabin and had employed muscles I don't usually use. Result? I was sore, I ached, and I complained.

"I feel terrible," I complained. "I had a rotten day."

Hans looked at me and inquired: "Rough?"

"Rough, indeed," I answered. "I put six squares of asphalt shingles on my sauna building."

"Roof," Hans mused and that was the end of the conversation.

I never though Hans was very bright. Oh, he didn't display such a high degree of ignorance that I considered him to be a danger to himself or others, but he certainly never impressed me as being PhD. material. Maybe I shouldn't have judged him so harshly. After all, my participation in most of our duck blind conversations was also limited to single words - words like "sit" or "heel" or "stay" or "fetch."

Hans was a German Shorthair hunting dog. He belonged to John and Karin Schmid. They had a cottage on Boulder Lake and during duck hunting week-ends, it was my occasional practice to spend the night sleeping on their couch. Hans would wake me in the morning before the alarm clock rang. Anxious and ready to go before there was any light in the sky, he loved to hunt ducks as much as I did.

While John and I might criticize each other's wives without incurring the other's ire, I placed too high a value on our friendship to mention my low opinion of his dog's intelligence quotient. Hans may have been a great duck dog but, otherwise, I was sure he was just plain dumb.

On command, Hans would plunge into the frigid November waters of that northern Wisconsin lake, take a hand signal and retrieve a bird with superb efficiency. That isn't necessarily a sign of intelligence. You've got to understand Hans was a German Shorthair. He didn't have the undercoat of a Chesapeake or a Lab. He didn't have enough body hair to offer much protection against the cold. Whenever he returned from a retrieve, he'd shiver and quiver and shake the whole blind.

After bringing back a duck, Hans would never shake off water while outside the blind. He'd always crawl inside and wait until John and I had been lulled into a false sense of security. Then he would shake and send a quart of icy droplets toward our exposed necks. His aim was good. After that performance, he'd begin his Olympic class shivering.

Hans had another interesting characteristic. He appeared to be unable to learn to swim around a decoy set. He preferred to return to the blind by way of the mathematical center of the layout. By the time he got back to land with one duck in his mouth, he'd have three decoys hopelessly entangled around his legs.

The routine was well established. We'd untangle him. Then we'd untangle the anchor lines. Then we'd wade out and re-set the blocks. Then we'd return to the blind and berate Hans for causing the mess. Hans would say nothing. Being reprimanded, he would put his muzzle on his paws and look up at us through sad, penitent eyes. Then he would shake ice water at us and I would quietly think: "Dumb Dog".

As Hans got older and grayer and increasingly arthritic, he still enjoyed retrieving ducks, but he couldn't take the cold as he once did. Before sunrise, John and I would walk to the shore blind. While Hans watched and shivered and supervised, we'd check the wind and find the underwater cement block that marked shotgun mid-range. We'd argue over the best set configuration and, finally, place the decoys and return to the blind.

The three of us would get in the blind and wait for 15 or 20 minutes for things to quiet down and for the sun to begin to color the eastern sky. When there is just enough light to be able to shoot, the temperature drops another five degrees and it's time to prepare for action. Waiting in the cold can be a miserable experience, but no one ever accused duck hunters of having too much sense. At this time, Hans would be nowhere in sight.

When the 12 gauges roared, however, things would be different. The adrenalin rush would erase any feeling of cold and Hans would appear from nowhere. He'd give us reproachful looks if we missed, but if there was a bird in the water, Hans would plunge in, retrieve the duck and wait for us to untangle him and reset the blocks. Then he'd shake the ice water on us and, a few minutes later, disappear.

It took me a long time to figure it out. Maybe I'm not too smart.

Whenever Hans became cold and uncomfortable, he would quietly leave the blind. He'd walk up the hill to the cottage and scratch at the door. Karin would let him in and he'd curl up on the rug before the fire while John and I sat in the blind - numb, dumb and freezing.

When he heard the shooting, Hans would get to the door as fast as his arthritis would allow. Karin would open the door and he'd come down to the blind to make the retrieve. Then he'd quietly go back uphill to a warm fire and some food.

As any frost bitten duck hunter would tell you, that is one smart dog.

Catch and Release

People in the media, as well as many other people who don't know anything about us, like to pass fishermen off on the unsuspecting public as contemplative, laid back, pipe smoking, gentle creatures, loathe to make critical comment about their fellow man and, in general, all-around good guys.

I suspect trout fishermen, in particular, stand in good report and are well recommended because of the prevalence of the "catch-and-release" policy adopted by many of them. Catch and release is, indeed, an admirable activity. Those who practice it understand you can't catch the fish again if you permanently take it out of the water.

In any event, the media considers the fisherman to be one of the most admirable of the sub-classes of the genus Homo sapiens. There are many who believe the media, for once, is accurately reporting the facts. So widespread is the positive public image of the fisherman that it is politically incorrect to suggest he is anything except a paragon of all of the known human virtues.

You can, therefore, imagine the consternation which developed when a contrary opinion was recently expressed. Brad Avery contends fishermen are scoundrels, destroyers of public morality and improper role models for our young. He claims trout fishermen, in particular, are an unwholesome and scurrilous lot, capable of exhibiting a depravity not experienced by civilized man since the attacks on the Roman Empire by the hordes of Attila the Hun.

Being personally addicted to the pursuit of trout, I found Brad's characterization of those who fish to be mildly disagreeable, but it got me to thinking. I had to take a bunch of aspirins to relieve the headache. Still, the frightening possibility that Brad might somehow be correct persisted. Sleep escaped me and it became clear. I had to do something about the matter.

Luckily, we live in a marvelous age where the answers to all important, earth-shattering questions can be determined by the results of polls. Newspapers carry them every day. Should all Congressmen be convicted and sent to prison? Take a poll. Is broccoli good to eat? Take a poll. Is it ecologically responsible to extend the deer hunting season for another week? Take a poll. Obviously, the question of whether or not trout fishermen are fine fellows can be determined by taking a poll.

I went to work on it and came up with a carefully worded inquiry. It posed a single question, to wit: After all is said and done, don't you really believe those fine people who fish are worthy and commendable? The person polled had the choice of checking the box marked "YES" or the box marked "POSSIBLY".

In order to satisfy myself that the poll was free from any and all bias, the proposed wording was submitted to the people who take the polls for both the Democrat and Republican National Committees. Their comments and suggestions were requested. To a man, those professionals agreed the wording of the submitted question was well calculated to receive a fair and unbiased response. Moreover, to insure an unprejudiced and impartial sampling of opinion, they recommended the questionnaire be sent only to those males who bought fishing licenses during the previous year.

And so it came to pass. The questionnaires were mailed

out, and soon the attached, self addressed, stamped postcards poured in. The results were quickly tabulated. You will be amazed and, surely, confounded by them.

Thirty Four percent of those polled answered: "Ha, Ha, Ha". Seventeen percent responded: "Don't be ridiculous". Forty two percent of the returned cards carried the penned notations: "No", "No, No", or "No, No, No." Sometimes those words were underlined and most of them were followed by three or four exclamation marks. The other Seven percent of the postcards contained dreadful obscenities and were disregarded.

Obviously the poll was skewed. Something had gone terribly wrong. The procedures adopted in taking the poll were reviewed and the error was discovered. It was the mailing date. The questionnaires were sent out the day before the opening of the fishing season. When delivered to the addressees, none of them were home. They were all on lakes or in trout water. It was not the fishermen, but their wives who had filled out and returned the answering postcards.

It is well established that fishermen's wives are in desperate need of the services of experienced psychiatrists. How else can you explain the fact of their decision to marry fishermen? Because of the poll's highly questionable validity, the results were never published. It was also considered prudent to make sure the results would never see the light of day.

In order to insure that secrecy, the poll results were marked "Urgent Report Requiring Immediate Attention" and sent to the federal government's Bureau of Fisheries. In accordance with the Bureau's established procedures, as soon as the report was received, it was filed away, unread.

To this day, no one knows the results of the polling. The file, still neglected, lays gathering mold in the basement of the one of the Bureau of Fisheries' Washington D. C. warehouses. Having thus cleverly hidden the poll from the public, I decided to find out just why Brad entertained such a low opinion of fishermen. A brief discussion with one of his erstwhile fishing buddies answered the question.

Earlier in the year, Brad and his friends were camped out on a trout stream. During their many previous fishing trips, Brad hadn't caught a fish large enough to give him bragging rights, but it wasn't for a lack of trying. He was usually the first one in the stream in the morning and the last one out of it in the evening.

This year it was different. The entire crew was in camp when Brad came sloshing out of the water and up to the camp fire. He was sporting a coprophagous grin and his companions knew something was up. As soon as he stood in the center of the circle of fishermen and wordlessly displayed a huge brook trout, they saw what was coming.

Brad was understandably proud of the fish. He was fully prepared to recount how he outsmarted it. He looked forward to repeating the story on every available occasion during the following two days of the trout fishing expedition.

Well, he didn't even get a chance to fire an opening salvo. As soon as he pulled the 18 incher from his creel and began to wave it around for all to admire, the other fishermen jumped all over him. He was roundly criticized for not returning the fish to the stream. Whenever he attempted to discuss the craftiness and intelligence he employed in beaching the trophy, he was immediately castigated for not having released it.

It's no wonder Brad considers "Catch and Release" to be nothing more than a mechanism for (a) keeping an honest man with unmistakable proof of the size of his fish from discoursing upon his fishing abilities, and, (b) for allowing scoundrels (i.e. fishermen to lie about the size of the ones they threw back.

A True Account

Deer hunters - when not talking about deer hunting - have been assigned an honesty quotient roughly equal to that of the general public. Translated into English, this means they tell the truth about 40 percent of the time. However, when discussing anything associated with the white tailed deer, the percentage of truthful statements issuing from the mouths of hunters can be expected to drop and approach absolute zero. Deer hunters have earned the reputation for being damnedably untruthful.

Prudent listeners have learned to take everything they say with a grain of salt (or, perhaps, a few kilos of the stuff). Still, there is the possibility, albeit remote, that a deer hunter will tell the truth. We are forever beset with the nagging suspicion that the one speaking to you may not be completely and universally dishonest. Regardless of the odds, he might be telling the truth

Jim Larson is a dedicated and consummate hunter of the white tailed deer. In a moment of weakness and, unwittingly I believe, he gave me an absolutely true account of what happened to him during last year's deer hunt in northern Wisconsin.

It was nearly the end of November. The gun season was in full swing and Jim was "still hunting." He was on one of his slow cross country jaunts, enjoying the woods and the exercise. As he walked through the second growth forest, he saw a stump that excited his curiosity. It was the remains of a huge white pine, the base of which was at least six feet in diameter.

Decaying stumps of that size can still be found in the

northern woods. This one was unique because it was charred, probably having met its demise via lightening or possibly during the famous Peshtigo fire. Because it was so charred, the outside of this stump hadn't disintegrated. It was still solid.

Even more striking, the top of the stump was nearly twelve feet above the forest's floor. As Jim approached the big stump for further investigation, he heard a scratching coming from within it. "This stump is hollow," he thought. "It contains a porcupine," he guessed.

Jim does not like porcupines. He claims they are hard to domesticate and dangerous to pet. They don't come when called and are not good to eat. They cannot be house broken and they chew up anything with even a trace of salt in it - like ax handles and outhouses.

In addition, some years earlier, a porcupine had developed a taste for the glue used in the plywood sheets forming the outer walls of Jim's cabin. During the winter one of them tried to eat every one of those sheets and met with a considerable degree of success.

Unable to identify the particular porcupine that attempted the outrage, all porcupines incurred Jim's displeasure. Since the wolverine and the pine marten have disappeared from many parts of the State it is said the porcupine has no natural enemies. Not true. Not as long as Jim Larson is alive.

Jim leaned his rifle against a nearby tree, picked up a stout branch and began to pound on the side of the stump. Being inside the stump was like being inside the kettle drum when the band plays Stars and Stripes Forever. It was no place to be and Jim knew the porky would soon crawl out. He recovered his rifle, held it at the ready and as soon as the head poked out from the top of the stump, he fired.

Jim immediately recognized his mistake. It wasn't a porcupine. It was a three hundred and fifty pound black bear.

The beast fell back down inside the twelve foot stump, dead as a liberal's conscience.

Jim needed a bear skin rug for his cabin so he decided to retrieve the carcass. He leaned a few limbs against the stump, made a make-shift ladder and managed to crawl to the top. As he bent over to peer down into the darkness, he lost his footing and fell into the stump and on top of the dead bear.

The interior walls of the stump were frozen and slippery and defied Jim's attempts to get a foothold and climb out. Trying to shimmy up the icy interior of a stump while carrying a 350 pound bear is an impossible task. You can see Larson's predicament. His only recourse was to cut a hole through the side of the stump and crawl out, dragging the bear behind him.

Some hunters carry hunting knives reminiscent of those huge Arabian cheese knives waived around by Shriners in their ceremonial parades. While a giant sized Bowie knife is very good for hand-to-hand combat, ever since the passage of the regressive legislation outlawing First Degree Murder there are very few of those kinds of battles going on. Jim doesn't believe in large knives. He carries a jack knife and it has performed every woodsy job assigned to it.

Jim found himself trapped inside a twelve foot stump, sitting on top of a dead bear and with a jack knife as his only tool. He embarked upon the task of cutting through the stump. He had made no discernable progress when he heard another scratching sound. This time it came from the outside of the hollow stump. The sounds began to move and it was clear something was climbing up the stump. When it reached the top, Jim found himself face to face with another bear.

Well, not exactly face to face. When the second black bear got to the opening at the top of the stump, it swung its hind end around and starting to back down into the hole. It wasn't a pretty sight. Moreover, Jim found himself in a dangerous predicament. Sitting at the bottom of the hollow stump on a dead bear, he was about to be crushed between two 350 pound black bears.

Jim planned his escape quickly and brilliantly. He locked his legs around the dead animal beneath him. Then, with his left hand he firmly grabbed the tail of the descending bear and, with his right, jabbed his jack knife into the beast's gluteus maximus.

This came as a real surprise to the bear who expected nothing more than a comfortable place to den up for its winter hibernation. It shot upwards like a Cape Canaveral missile bound for Mars - pulling both Jim and the dead bear out of the stump and into the full light of day.

Now you may harbor a suspicion about the truth of this story. I'll admit I did. However, when I was moved to exclaim: "Bull Shoot" (or something like that), Jim produced the jack knife he used to facilitate his escape. In the face of such overwhelming evidence, I became convinced the tale was, in fact, entirely true.

Extinction

Most of the out-of-doors types in this grand Republic lead rather non-combative lives. Our philosophy of life can be boiled down to a single statement, to-wit: We didn't cause any of these problems. We probably won't be able to solve any of these problems. We just live here.

It doesn't make much sense to rational people to team up with some cleverly acronymed group and contribute money which could otherwise be sensibly used to buy fishing tackle, shotguns and camping equipment. To send money to some Committee that claims it will use the funds to Protect Our Right to Arm Bears or to Shave The Whales or some other such laudable purpose seems ridiculous. Especially when a closer examination of their Annual Statements shows most of the contributions will be used to pay for fund raising expenses and salaries

Most of us think it is a clear indication of a vacancy in the brain department for anyone to spend a weekend during fishing season marching around a building, lugging a sign, yelling slogans and, in general, carrying on in a raucous and contentious manner.

Oh, sure, there have been times in our lives when we became convinced we had to grab a banner and rush up a hill shouting "Excelsior". Looking back at it now, it is more than extremely doubtful we changed the course of human events or made the world a better place. In our maturity, we have learned to be cautious about supporting anything simply because it sounds good or has a clever motto.

We have learned there is a lot of hypocrisy loose in the land. When the United Nations (United ??) (Nations??) announced the bug causing Smallpox had been eliminated from the face of the earth, a national chorus of "hurrah" ascends into the stratosphere. The same people who quiver with delight over the extinction of the Smallpox bug will fight like Tasmanian Devils to keep other bugs alive. They'll form societies and raise more money than the beer lobby to stop the construction of an industrial plant because its presence might injure some blind minnow living deep in an underground cave.

A moment's thought will convince anyone with an IQ larger than that of Koko the Gorilla that some forms of life deserve - nay - demand extinction. I'm not just referring to homicidal maniacs, child molesters, U S Senators and the like. I mean a whole bloomin' species - from A to Izard. Any right thinking citizen will agree.

Let me explain it this way: When you are wandering around in some covert in search of a grouse, I'm sure you are glad - truly glad - there is no Tyrannosaurus Rex watching you and licking its chops. Consider how happy you should be, secure in the knowledge that you will not have to try to stop the charges of that beast with nothing more than a load of 7 1/2 chilled bird shot.

If the balance of nature has been upset by the extinction of large fanged predators that, were they were still alive, would be sneaking about trying to make a meal of upland bird hunters, so be it. I won't complain, but I won't contribute to any group who wants to find Tyrannosaurus Rex DNA and clone them back into existence.

If the Pterodactyl and the Smallpox bug can vanish from the earth without signaling the end of all life as we know it, or even significantly disfiguring the surviving ecosystems, doesn't it seem reasonable to assume the destruction of other forms of life can occur without destroying the planet? Of course it does and a number of examples to prove that thesis come to mind. The earth would be better off if a number of its inhabitants were knocked off. Mankind is one of them.

I'm not recommending Mankind's extinction just now. I'm in good health. Perhaps in another 50 years or so, wiping out the Homo sapiens should deserve serious consideration.

However, without mental reservation of any kind, I can recommend the immediate and total annihilation of one critter and all of its relatives. Mother Nature must have been drunk when she created the wood tick. When the first Congress for the Elimination of a Species convenes, I intend to jump up and nominate the wood tick. I'm sure the "Ayes" will have it by the widest of margins.

What earthly purpose do they serve? I've never seen a fish or an animal or a bird eat one. There's not enough substance to them to contend they offer any beneficial fertilization of the soil when they die. I suppose it can be argued they perform an admirable function by carrying Lyme's disease and Rocky Mountain Fever, thereby helping to alleviate the world's terrible overpopulation problem, but I'm willing to overlook it.

Doing my very best to be charitable and give it the benefit of every doubt, I join the vast majority of outdoorsmen in considering wood ticks to be worthless, miserable, rotten, no-good, unproductive, contemptible, vile, unclean, offensive and blood sucking (deleted).

For over forty years I've tried to find a good way to remove the little (deleted) without having them leave part of their head and/or their toxins inside my hide and leaving me with an itchy lump.

I've put detergent on them. Ticks breathe through their skin. When the detergent covers them, they are supposed to unbite and pull their heads out, all by themselves. Tommy rot! I've tried screwing them out - both clockwise and counter clockwise. Sorry. No help. I've tried burning them off with sulphury stick matches. Did it help? No way, José. I can show you a very ugly scar on my left rear cheek in proof thereof. Nothing works. I always end up with a hard, red, itching welt to show for my efforts.

Well - no more Mister Nice Guy. I'm out to exterminate them and I ask for your support. It's going to take a lot of work and a lot of bucks to get the job done. It's a terribly difficult undertaking. Trying to kill them one by one is a program destined for failure. Each lady wood tick produces about five thousand eggs. Even if every one of us went into the woods, collected a handful and killed every one of them, wood tick reproduction would outdistance us.

Perhaps one of our county's quasi-environmentalist groups could be talked into spending some of the money they've earmarked for fund raising and, instead, hire a bunch of scientists and tell them to develop a way to guarantee the continued existence of the wood tick. Then we could do the exact opposite of what the scientists have proposed and guarantee the extinction of the little (deleted).

Aging

There's a lot of absolute nonsense floating about the universe and a high percentage of it has to do with the aging process. Those of us who, through the exercise of good judgment, the application of common sense and the ability to avoid being shot by some irate husband, have attained 70 + years of age can recognize much of that foolishness.

Those of you who have not had the good sense to get to be 70 don't have the experience to be able to separate fact from fiction. You all lack basic education. Fear not, youngsters. You are about to learn some solid facts - whether you like it or not.

For one thing, most of you hold the mistaken opinion that a lifetime of smoking cigars will have an adverse effect upon one's ability to charge up the hills while driving deer. Pure hogwash - but I can understand how you might come to that conclusion if you were not cognizant of the plate theory of continental land mass drift.

Any competent geologist will tell you plates have joined to form the surface of the earth. They are all floating on a sea of liquid magma. Ever since the earth cooled off, the shifting of those plates has caused the world's surface to move and, when they collide, to rise. This phenomenon has formed the Himalayas, the Rockies and, in particular, they have affected the immediate area surrounding the place where I do my deer hunting.

The obvious result of plate movement is to make the hills much steeper than they were twenty five years ago when I could leap around on them like a gazelle. Since the hills are now higher and steeper than they used to be, I must occasionally pause to catch my breath when I am called upon to be a driver.

When I presented these facts to a youngster of the tender age of 45 during last years deer hunt, he made rude snorts and sounds, clearly indicating disbelief. Hah! What does he know? His senses are not as good as mine. I happen to know his hearing is so bad he can't even hear the ringing in his own ears. You and I both know everyone has ringing in his ears. Don't we?

Mosquitoes

There are folks who claim mosquitoes are absolutely useless and should be scourged from the face of the earth. This, of course, is pure nonsense. Mosquitoes, like the Homo sapiens, have both good and bad qualities. The good traits of a species justify its continued existence. We must be willing to overlook the not-so-good characteristics.

As an example of the mosquito's good qualities, without it, there would be no yellow fever, malaria, elephantiasis or Nile disease and the overpopulation problem the world now faces would be greatly exacerbated. We must consider this and the mosquito's other praiseworthy qualities before peremptorily pushing the insect into extinction

Some of my friends seem to be preoccupied with sex. They tell me mosquito larvae are the result of mosquito sex. I don't know about such things. I have to take their word for it. Presuming my sex-obsessed fishing companions are correct, a number of conclusions logically follow. Without mosquitoes, there would be no mosquito larvae. Without mosquito larvae, trout would lose an important food source.

Studies by competent biologists tell us there is a dramatic decrease in the number of pups in wolf litters whenever there is a decrease in the supplies of the foods wolves like to eat. If trout are anything like wolves, in the absence of their mosquito larvae food source, the size of trout litters could be expected to dramatically decrease. If trout fishing went to hell, fishermen would become morose and despondent. With no place to go on weekends, they would spend their spare time at home being helpful to their wives.

The result would be domestic strife and a sky rocketing increase in the number of divorce actions. The increase in the number of divorce petitions (the stuff lawyers feed upon) would result in larger litters of attorneys - markedly expanding the numbers now infesting the land.

As a direct result of the alimony awards, the divorced fishermen would have to stop buying fishing lures, rods and reels and lines, boats, outboard motors and multi-bladed Swiss army type fishing tools.

The manufacturers of all that stuff would go bankrupt. Widows, dependant upon dividends from their stock, would become destitute. Large segments of the population would be thrown out of work. The increased costs of unemployment compensation and welfare payments would strain the federal budget and give the liberals in Congress an opportunity to increase FICA withholding and income taxes to even higher levels.

The men who still had jobs would scream: "Taxation without representation". Actually, no taxpayer has ever been represented in Washington D.C. A tax revolt and a march on the nation's capitol would follow. Someone would fire a gun. The FBI, the Drug and Alcohol people and the rest of the various federal agencies authorized to kill citizens, would fire back. Revolution. Calamity. Catastrophe. Ruin. General annoyance.

And all of this would be the result of getting rid of the mosquito.

On the other hand, there are those who believe such a price is one reasonably people should be willing to pay. They seek the establishment of government grants to study the feasibility of nuclear devices especially designed to kill mosquitoes and nothing else.

This is the sort of thing that drives the Animal Rights community nuttier than usual. Anyone who would kill a living creature, the Animal Rightsers contend, is a murderer. He should be prosecuted by the District Attorney for violation of the State's criminal statutes that take a dim view of homicide.

The people who hold this view live, mostly, in apartments in downtown urban centers, although some inhabit asylums for the mentally feeble. Like most bunny huggers, the Animal Rightser's association with the woods has been tenuous at best. They have seldom, if even, found themselves in an environment where mosquitoes occur.

Most campers and hunters and fishers pay no attention to either of the two above described extremist views. We adopt a moderate middle ground position. Live and let live is our motto. If a mosquito stays at least three feet from us, we won't kill it. However, if its vampirish tendencies can't resist the high quality of our blood and if it has the temerity to come within swatting distance, then it has no one to blame but itself if we squish it.

The mosquito needs blood to produce eggs. Male mosquitoes, I am told by my sex-obsessed associates, do not produce eggs. This explains why it is the female mosquito and not the male that goes after you. Communicating with a female is not easy. Likewise, communicating with a female mosquito is not easy, but we in the moderate center have tried. The humanitarianism of this centrist view is shown by our attempts to give lady mosquitoes a fair warning. They are in mortal danger if they approach us.

When grandfather was a lad, the warning took the form of smoke producing smudges. He'd put grass over the coals of a campfire. The resulting smoke would tell the lady mosquito she was not wanted in the area. The smudge program had some drawbacks. For instance; when you are walking down a trout stream, it is very difficult to carry a smudge pot in one hand and try to fish with the other. Building a smudge fire in the bottom of a wooden boat while lake fishing has been tried and found to produce unintended results.

Today we continue to struggle with the mosquito problem. The chemical companies have come up with various lotions, salves and sprays. If we douse ourselves with their products, they assure us mosquitoes will keep their distance. Some of these concoctions come in canisters that will help destroy the world's protective ozone cover. Some work well - for ten minutes. Others smell very nice. They do more than keep lady mosquitoes away. They also attract lady human beings.

If you think you've got a problem trying to fly fish and carry a smoke smudge pot at the same time, try wading a stream and casting when some woman is hanging onto your neck, rubbing against you, squirming, splashing her feet in the water and generally making a nuisance of herself.

I have a solution to the problem. Lay a couple of strips of bacon out in the sun. Put cheese cloth over them to keep the flies away. After a few days the bacon will become ripe and ready for use. Before entering the stream, rub the rancid bacon over all exposed areas. The smell will keep all females - mosquitoes and otherwise - at a respectful distance. It might attract bear, but you can't have everything, now can you?

The Ascension of Ed

Ed was a worm fisherman, For the benefit of the purist fly fisherman and for the enlightenment of the unsophisticated non-fisherman, a worm fisherman is one who uses worms for bait - not one who fishes for worms. Ed liked to fish for speckled trout on small streams where patience and finesse are necessary if one is to be successful. In this context, people who don't fish consider the words "patience and finesse" to mean "lazy and deceitful".

Ed wasn't really lazy, I guess. However, a certain amount of guile and cunning is a part of every fisherman's paraphernalia and I suppose you might call Ed deceitful.

You're damned right you can call Ed deceitful. A few years ago, he kept bringing back double handfuls of good sized brook trout and I asked him where he caught them. He told me. He gave me the names of five streams. I knew he was lying so I spent the summer fighting through the tag alders of the streams Ed didn't mention. I fished every stream he had been know to fish - every stream except the ones where he told me he had caught the big ones. Then I learned Ed had told me the truth.

There's deceit for you. By the time I learned that scoundrel had not lied, Ed's best fishing hole had been posted and a herd of cows were using the next best one as a watering hole. The fishing had been ruined. Of course, Ed became very unpopular when the word got out that he had not lied. The older fishermen berated him for telling the truth. It was a bad precedent for a fisherman to tell the truth. It sets a terrible example for the children.

Unfortunately for Ed, the minister was a devout trout fisherman. He figured if fishing was good enough for Saint Peter, it was good enough for him. Having an indefensible belief in the basic goodness of mankind, the minister thought Ed might tell him the truth - he being a man of the cloth and all that. But Ed had learned his lesson. He told the truth once and all he got was a scolding from the other trout fishermen.

The good pastor spent an afternoon stumbling around in a cedar swamp in search of a spring hole which, Ed had assured him, contained a multitude of brookies - all over twelve inches long. He found only a mosquito marsh containing no open water and Ed was on his way to eternal damnation.

The following Sunday morning the sermon dealt with people who lied about where they caught trout. The minister concluded they were nothing but a bunch of damned liars, motivated by unclean spirits - perhaps even by the devil himself. Such a man, the minister thundered, should stop fishing on Sunday mornings and spend more time in church contemplating his sins. Everyone knew he was talking about Ed.

Like most of the members of the trout fishing fraternity, Ed spent his May through September Sunday mornings splashing around in small streams. In Ed's case, the grouse, the ducks and the deer absorbed his October and November Sundays - but he never missed a Christmas or an Easter service. Ed's wife went to church religiously and on all occasions prayed mightily for his immortal soul.

The minister remained obdurate and abundantly irritated. He insisted Ed mend his ways, reduce some of his lying and improve his church attendance record. None of those sugges- tions attracted Ed's interest. He paid no attention to any of the proposals and some of the Elders threatened to remove his name from the church rolls. The stage was set for high drama. Community opinion quickly polarized. Fists fights broke out between the pagans and Christians. The battle lines were drawn and there was no middle ground.

One part of the population backed the minister. Ed and his kind, they contended, were responsible for the breakdown of morality visited on the nation. They felt it had to be a sin for anyone to have as much fun as Ed was having when he fished for brook trout.

The others group consisted of trout fishermen, bass fishermen, pan fishermen, pantheists, and the owners of bait shops and sporting goods stores. They insisted Ed was no worse than anyone who attended church regularly. Because he always lied about where he caught those big trout, Ed's defenders agreed that he (like the church attendees) would probably go to hell. Still, they claimed he had a Constitutional right to fish for trout.

Ed disregarded the controversy swirling around him. He gave no interviews, made no appearance at any of the rallies and busied himself with his usual preoccupation - fishing for brook trout and lying about it.

On a Sunday morning last May, a group of canoeists were busy screwing up the trout fishing on the South Branch. They were witnesses to a strange happening. As they paddled around a bend in the river, they heard a man calling out the name of Deity. Then they saw him on his knees at the base of a huge White Ash tree. They watched as he clasped his hands before him and gazed upwards in prayer. They recognized the man. It was Ed.

That tree, they reported, grew at the river's edge. With roots in the water as well as in the shore and with branches extending high up into the air, the tree seemed to unite the heavens, the earth and the waters.

Before the sun had set, the canoeists' story was known by everyone in town. The minister and Ed, however, had no opportunity for conversation about the fisherman's return to religion. On the very next day Ed was struck by lightning. He died only a few feet away from the magnificent tree he had used as an altar.

Ed's funeral was well attended. The minister described him as a man of firm religious conviction - a man who recognized the presence of Deity everywhere - especially in the woods and on the streams.

* * * * *

Ed floated a worm down past an undercut bank and when he felt the tugs, he dropped the tip of his rod slightly and gave the fish some slack line. When he set the hook, the fish took the line into the roots of a tree growing at the side of the river and the leader snapped. Ed tied a new leader to his line and as he walked along the bank, he looked down and saw his trout. The broken leader had tangled and caught in the tree's roots. The trout was still hooked onto the line.

The fish was still frisky, darting this way and that. Ed never carried a net so he plunged his arm deeply into the water, planning to grab the fish or the leader. The springtime water was frigid and as it covered his upper arm, an involuntary "Oh, God" escaped his lips.

At this moment two canoes came around a bend in the river. Ed quickly pulled his arm from the water and hoped the canoeists would believe he had been praying. He wasn't going to let anyone guess this was the precise spot where big brook trout regularly convened.

State v. Manley

Sylvester Manley lived in the Upper Peninsula. He spent a good deal of time in the forests harvesting fallen hardwood trees under authorizations granted by the Michigan Department of Natural Resources. Manley would search the forests for hardwoods tops and blow downs. He'd cut and split the wood into appropriate sizes. What he didn't use to keep his own cabin warm he would sell to others who needed it to keep their places snug and comfortable.

Some people wondered how Manley could live so well on the pittance he made by selling fireplace wood. The answer was simple. Manley had other sources of income. Because of his woodsy occupations, Manley knew where the Ruffed Grouse population was concentrated, where beaver had dammed up trout streams and where other wild life and deer were abundant.

If a flatlander (a Michigander who lived in Lower Michigan) spent the deer season getting drunk in some U P cabin, he would be interested in bringing a buck back home to prove he had been hunting. Manley would sell him the deer. During the spring and summer, fancy Detroit social clubs would prepare venison for their members. Guess where they got the meat. Manley also traded in animal skins. He'd trap them legally, if convenient, and sell them to dealers - law abiding ones, if convenient.

The local game warden was crafty, but not as crafty as Sylvester Manley. Manley was never caught although he was suspected of violating almost every fish and game regulation on the books. It was purely by accident when the warden discovered him baiting a mink trap with rancid meat. Though the trapping season was open, the warden became curious and surreptitiously followed him. He caught Manley cutting more bait from the body of a dead and skinned out wolf carcass, hidden in a camouflaged, underground cache.

Manley was arrested and charged with killing a gray wolf - one of the species protected by the Michigan DNR.

Manley's attorney argued for dismissal of the charge. The State of Michigan, he pointed out, issued Manley a permit to cut wood. A licensee working in an area of government timber land, he argued, fell under the Michigan Safe Place statutes. The employer (in this case, the State of Michigan) had to provide Sylvester Manley with a safe place to work.

The woods where Manley was authorized to work were known to be frequented by wolves and bears and other vicious beasts. Manley could not be held responsible for any actions flowing out of the State's own negligence in failing to provide a Safe Place for him to perform his duly authorized labors. Manley's attorney threatened to sue the State for damages and moved for a dismissal. The judge immediately denied the motion.

There are those who believe the judge didn't understand the lawyer's argument. The Defendant's Motion to Dismiss contained a number of two and even three syllable words. In addition, the members of the local Bar Association were well aware of the judge's penchant for falling asleep during argument. When roused into consciousness, he would automatically and loudly call out: "Motion Dismissed". It saved him from embarrassment and the decision was usually right, anyway.

With the denial of his Motion, Manley's attorney entered a

plea of not guilty by reason of self defense and the case was set for a jury trial. Local antagonism toward the DNR, coupled with sympathy for the man who had shown so many of them where to hunt grouse, led everyone to conclude the jury would return a verdict of Not Guilty if there was any credible substance to the Self Defense plea.

State v Manley received widespread publicity. Curiosity seekers filled the city's lone motel. Venison burgers were sold on the street. Tree worshippers lectured on the evils of cutting into trees. A delegation from the Shave the Wolves Society was run out of town. In this festive atmosphere, the case came to trial.

The DA put in his evidence and rested. Then Sylvester Manley took the stand.

Manley testified he had been cutting deadfalls when he heard terrified shrieks and cries for help. He took his axe and ran toward the source of the screaming. He came upon a red haired woman closely pursued by a huge wolf with bared teeth and snarling in a ferocious manner. He told how the slavering beast then attacked him and how he killed it on the spot. Manley's testimony held up quite well during the DA's cross examination though he was forced to admit that he skinned out the animal and used its meat to bait his mink traps.

To support Manley's testimony, his attorney called Ms. Hood to the stand

Ms Hood was the young, red hair woman Manley claimed to have saved during the wolf attack. "Little Red", as the members of her motorcycle gang called her, was a real doll. She weighed in at about 120 well proportioned pounds. She testified she was carrying a basket of goodies to her grandmother's house when the attack occurred.

The judge did not fall asleep during her testimony. He changed his position a few times to get a better view of her as she crossed and re-crossed her legs while seated in the witness chair. The jury followed suit.

Little Red testified she ran through the woods, petrified with fear as she fought off the wolf with rocks and tree branches. She claimed she was nearing the end of her ability to defend herself when Manley appeared and dispatched the beast with his axe.

Little Red's testimony was shaken by the DA's cross examination. Her own answers as well as the information given by the State's rebuttal witnesses destroyed Sylvester Manley's defense.

Witnesses characterized Little Red as a wild motorcycle freak who often rode with a group known as the Wolf Pack. The Wolf Pack gang could be recognized by their trade mark - wolf skin jackets. Little Red got her own wolf skin jacket only a few days before Manley was arrested. She was pleased with the jacket and was overheard saying she was going to give Manley a bonus of two six packs of beer.

In her cross-examination, the young red head admitted she was carrying two six packs and not a basket full of goodies for her grandmother. Little Red's credibility was destroyed when asked why her grandmother wasn't in court to substantiate her testimony. Visibly shaken, she finally said her granny couldn't testify because the wolf ate her.

That did it. The jury found all of her testimony to be incredible and Manley's Self Defense argument collapsed. The jury was out for two hours before returning a verdict of Guilty. It was later reported they had elected a foreman and found Manley guilty in five minutes. The rest of the time they faked it in order to be able to send out for a fried chicken dinner at the county's expense.

Little Red Riding Hood was charged and convicted of being an accessory before, during and after the fact.

The Ruffed Grouse

People who survive the summer months and have witnessed the autumnal equinox rejoice in the advent of October. There are many causes of this annual jubilation. The color of the woods changes from drab greens to happier reds and yellows. The sounds of migrating geese are heard again. The children are in school and have changed the target of their harassments from their parents to their teachers. The grass stops growing and the lawn mower can be shoved into a corner of the garage, there to rest undisturbed until next April. (June?)

However, the most important reason for the celebration is the opening of the Ruffed Grouse hunting season.

Many people are addicted to the hunting of the grouse. Some of them read. Some of them buy outdoor sports magazines. In an effort to cozy up to them and develop a few invitations to join hunts, the Editor has suggested (i.e. insisted) a scholarly and learned treatise be produced for the enlightenment of the grouse hunter. All right, I'll play his silly game. Brace yourself.

According to the U. S. Department of Agriculture Poster # 50 (BI), the first edition of which was issued on July 10, 1931, there was no open season for the hunting of grouse in Wisconsin. Now, some three quarters of a century later, as soon as the September page is torn from the calendar, the rational inhabitants of that State busily engage themselves in preparing for forays into Ruffed Grouse covert. (There aren't too many irrational people in Wisconsin. A lot of them have been sent to Washington, D. C.)

Few people know the reason why the hunting of the grouse has been allowed. The failure to include that information within the basic curricula of our grade and high schools is yet another indication of the terrible condition of our country's educational system. Thousands of bird shooter-aters spend countless nights unable to sleep, tossing and turning as they struggled to find an answer to the question: "Why did the federal government decide to allow the Ruffed Grouse to be hunted?"

Well, comrades, your torture goes not unnoticed. You will soon enjoy that deep, serene and dreamless sleep enjoyed by those very, very few of us who have an absolutely clear conscience. Here, for the first time, the answer to your vexing question is revealed. Please don't thank me for providing this boon to civilization and ending your sleepless nights. I hate opening mail filled with effusive praise. A simple statue at some attractive location at the State capitol will be sufficient.

One of the clues to the reason behind the opening of the Ruffed Grouse hunting season is found within the Latin name assigned by the academicians to the Ruffed Grouse - the Bonasa Umbellus Umbellus.

The astute observer will notice the bird's middle and last names are the same. It is not an uncommon practice for parents to use the wife's maiden name as their offspring's middle name. The name Bonasa Umbellus Umbellus, said the federal zoologists, clearly suggests the birds have adopted that practice. Those same federal zoologists were led to the obvious conclusion that there was a lot of interbreeding going on in the Ruffed Grouse community.

We all know the results of interbreeding. The Czarovitch's hemophilia and the Hapsburgs' lips are examples of what happened when the Romanovs and the Hapsburgs kept marrying their own relatives. The unfortunate results of marrying first cousins can be witnessed by reviewing the miserable quality of the politicians who come from West Virginia or Arkansas.

Well, anyway, when this Umbellus Umbellus intermarriage situation became general public knowledge, it really hit the fan. The media had a field day. Reports of Ruffed Grouse immorality appeared in the newspaper headlines. Sermons denouncing the bird were delivered throughout the land. The media's newscasters decried the practice and blamed it on a vast right grouse wing conspiracy.

In California, many of the commentators defended the Ruffed Grouse. They claimed the bird had merely adopted an alternative life style and should not be castigated. In Massachusetts, state legislators contended Ruffed Grouse were consenting adults and it was nobody's business what close relatives did in the privacy of their own nests. Their State Supreme Court upheld a law legalizing all Ruffed Grouse marriages.

In Washington D.C. (in support of their efforts to make sure the federal budget doesn't come close to being balanced) Congressmen insisted on mega-dollar government grants to study the grouse's sex habits. Various studies were undertaken and a new government bureau was created. A number of defeated politicians were removed from the welfare rolls when they got jobs in the new bureau..

After a careful review of the bureau's studies, Congressmen discovered they would win more votes than they would lose if they took action. As a result, they passed a law declaring the Ruffed Grouse's behavior to be immoral, indecent and a crime against the peace and dignity of the United States of America.

Being a Ruffed Grouse became a crime and the penalty for

committing that crime was death by firing squad. That penalty, however, was limited only to perpetrators captured between October 1 and January 30 of the year. (Occasionally the dates are changed.)

And thus began the Grouse Hunting Season.

* * * * *

During my extensive research of the Bonasa Umbellus Umbellus, certain heretofore unreported facts were developed.

In the Latin language, 'Bonasa" translates as "bison", and "umbellus" means "neck ruff". The naturalist who first discovered the Ruffed Grouse and assigned its Latin name suffered from two embarrassing impediments. One of them was his pronounced stammer. A transcription of the conversation which took place when he first sighted the bird follows:

"Hey-hey, Otis. Di-did you hear that lloud thumping s-sound? L-like a two-two cylinder gas-gas engine? W-well it was a bir-bird. No ki-kidding. It t-took off practically under my fee-feet. Sus-scared the living bejaysus out of me. It l-looked a l-lot like a bi-bison with a feathery ruff- ruffed neck. I th-think I'll call-call it the Bonasa Umbellus Umbellus."

Our stammering naturalist meant to name the bird "the Bonasa Umbellus", but due to his stuttering, he repeated the last word.

The naturalist's second impediment was his inability to hold his liquor. Most of us are able to tell the difference between a bird and a buffalo. The ones who can't have been convicted and sentenced to serve five year terms of soft labor as Directors of State Departments of Natural Resources.

Logic

At first I thought it was only What's-Her-Name, but upon closer examination, I discovered there are a lot of forces on this planet which oppose everything reasonable with an uncompromising and mulish obstinacy. I don't mean just the Mayor and the Common Council, either. I mean it is every-where.

The perversity of inanimate objects is well recognized. The zipper on the inside pocket of your fly vest will only stick when the flies in the box stored deep therein are a perfect match of the hatch coming off the river. The knife in the cabin is not sharp enough to cut the green pepper, but it will open a great and frightful gash in your thumb.

Wild life occasionally will display the same irrational and stubborn resistance to logic and order. You identify the Ephemerella Subvaria perfectly and select a Hendrickson variant that looks so natural, real insects try to mate with it as you tie it to the leader. Then, you carefully creep to a position where you can reach four feeding stations and you present the fly in a brilliant manner - again - and again - and again. You fail to coax so much as a short hit from the natural, real trout everywhere engaging in a shark-like feeding frenzy.

Then some joker comes plowing through the underbrush, falls into the stream above the pool, gets up and in less time than it takes to exclaim, "Well, I'll be a --- of a -----", he'll pull out three in the 14-16 inch class. He'll use a Rat Faced McDougal - a fly that looks as much like an Ephemerella Subvaria as Teddy Kennedy looks like Sharon Stone.

64

And is the government rational? If you answer that question in the affirmative, someone will throw a net over you and haul you off to an asylum to be kept in constant restraint in a padded cell and under heavy sedation.

The fact that your elected Congressional Representatives are silly shouldn't come as any shock. What defies all logic is the fact that you keep re-electing them. Perhaps you are the one who needs the attentions of a competent psychiatrist.

Ryan Mitchell, a Trout Unlimited activist, has made an in-depth study of that subject. He thinks there is a reasonable explanation for the phenomena. Ryan says we elect people to Congress as a mechanism for ridding the community of undesirables. He claims they are re-elected and remain at the State or Federal capitol until they pay their debt to society and prove they deserve another chance. Then on the date of the next election, they will be defeated at the polls and can again return to their homes.

Listen, friends, if people used their heads in a logical manner, the immediate decrease in courtroom litigation and the reduction in the demand for attorneys would cause the universities to close their law schools and thousands of lawyers would be forced to shut the doors of their offices and seek honest employment.

Now you know me, I'm a temperate and placid type, not given to outbursts of hyperbole. Under normal circumstances I wouldn't get upset about the lack of logic in the Republic, but I've had a few bad days and the clouded perception of some of my neighbors has finally gotten to me.

You see, What's-Her-Name and most of my neighbors have cats. Somehow or other, I've developed a bad reputation concerning the sneaky and untrustworthy little critters. Even if I only look like I'm going to take a good healthy kick at one of them, some lady is apt to come running out of her house, berate me, scream at me and rescue the animals before I can take a shot at it.

I began to think about all this and decided to be good to What's-Her-Name's cat and do something nice for my skittish, four-footed, bewhiskered friends. My motives were pure and unassailable. I was trying to do the cats a good turn.

Now then, everyone knows fresh meat is much better for cats than the canned or the dry packaged stuff. So, I knocked down our bird feeder and rebuilt it about 18 inches from the ground. I thought this would give What's-Her-Name's cats a hunting advantage (and cut down on the cost of feeding it).

Well, friends, that simple act of kindness caused quite a bit of excitement on the home front. A neighbor saw our cat, Jaws, closing in on a sparrow and it didn't take long before all the ladies in the vicinity were running over my lawn, retrieving their kitties from under the shrubbery, waving their arms and yelling to frighten the birds away and making a lot of uncomplimentary comments about me. I didn't think women knew those words.

I know they reported me to the Audubon Society and if it weren't for the fact that I have something on the District Attorney, I'm sure they would have persuaded him to bring charges of conspiracy to commit murder of starlings, or maybe, assault with a deadly cat.

Just try to be nice and see where it gets you. All of these people were 32nd degree cat lovers and suddenly, without reason, they turned on me and became rabid bird lovers. This inconsistency is another display of the basically perverse and illogical nature of the universe.

Even their inconsistency will, I'm sure, be inconsistent. I'll bet a million all of my neighbors will revert to being fanatic cat fanciers just as soon as they learn I'm trying to support their current aberration and plan to help out the little birdies by importing some owls to cut down on the local cat population. Just you wait and see if I'm not right.

Save the Environment

The gun control people are convinced the licensing of hand guns will reduce the incidence of violent crimes because guns are the cause of the violent crimes. I wonder if they are equally convinced automobiles are the cause of highway fatalities and, therefore, the licensing of automobiles will reduced the incidence of those deaths.

When forced into a corner, some gun controllers will admit the one who pulls the trigger is the one who causes the crime, but they still insist licensing the gun owner will reduce crime. Somehow they have greater difficulty in arguing the licensing of the automobile owner has reduced highway fatalities.

There are a lot of very strange concepts floating around. There are people running loose in this Republic who believe they can save the planet by reducing the emission of dangerous gasses through the mechanisms of placing scrubbers on smoke stacks and destroying all internal combustion engines. Some even spend their time trying to figure out a way to control the methane emitted from the south ends of north-bound cows.

There are others - the Nature Conservancy, the Ducks Unlimited and the Trout Unlimited folks, for example - who are convinced the major menace to the future of life on earth is much broader. They define that danger as the destruction of the kind of habitat required by living things. They direct their efforts to producing wetlands, fixing up trout streams and buying lands to be used for the exclusive use of birds and animals.

I support the Nature Conservancy, the DU and the TU folks, but I must admit it - all of them, as well as the gun control and noxious emission people, are on the wrong track. A moment's reflection will reveal the true culprit. People use guns to rob banks and commit crimes. People get loaded and drive automobiles. People drain wetlands so they can build condos and live, cheek to jowl, with their neighbors. People create toxic waste by making demands that can be filled only through the use of chemicals with long half-lives.

As the world's population explodes, people's need to use more of the resources of the world also explodes. They need more land and more lumber from more trees to build more houses. They need more food - more wheat and soy beans and oats which requires more chemical fertilizers. They need more meat which demands more cattle (producing more methane) and more grazing land. More women require more baby seal and leopard fur coats.

To phrase the problem delicately: It is people who are destroying the world. There are too damned many of them.

During the 1930s, the federal government adopted an interesting program to help the farmer work his way out of the Great Depression. It was a simple matter of supply and demand. There was too much farm product on the market. Limit the amount of farm product, they contended, and prices will rise. Prosperity will return to the farmer. He will stay on the farm instead of piling into an old truck, heading for California and giving John Steinbeck raw material for The Grapes of Wrath. So, the Agriculture Department paid the farmers to kill every third pig and plow under every other row of corn.

There is a lesson to be learned from that 1930s AAA experiment. I propose we apply it to our present day efforts to save Mother Earth. I propose all environmental protection enthusiasts write to their Washington politicians and insist on the establishment of a federally funded program designed to kill every other person in the United States.

The effects of this program will be immediate and dramatic. Half of the nation's automobiles will no longer be used. Over night, our dependence on foreign oil will disappear. In Los Angeles, smog will be cut in half. The inhabitants of that city may suddenly be able to see and find their way out of that terrible place. The number of drunken drivers who aim their vehicles at us will also be reduced by fifty percent. Moreover, since half of all automobiles will have been removed from the highways, the rest of us will have twice as much room to dodge them.

The advantages of such a Population Reduction Program extend far beyond our oil and our highway death toll crises. The beneficial effects on violent crime should be recognized. Only half of the people shooters will be around. They can be expected to kill only half as many people. Actually, it will be less than that. Instead of the drive-by shooter indiscriminately throwing lead at 12 people in some overcrowded neighborhood apartment, there will be only six there with more space between them for missing.

Only half the paper will be necessary to produce all of that very interesting and essential junk mail which floods us day after day. With fewer trees being harvested, the National Forests will be saved. Watersheds will be larger and better. There will be more leaves for the photosynthesis process to produce more oxygen from carbon dioxide.

Food consumption will be cut in half. Only half the farm land will need to be cultivated. The other half will fall into disuse and provide excellent cover for pheasants and quail. Only half of the wastes and chemicals people use will find their way into our fishing lakes and trout streams. With half their clients plowed under, half the attorneys will have to close their offices and, for the first time, seek productive employment.

The list of advantages of finishing off half of the population is a long one. Just think of the salutary effects on our political system. The House of Representative and the Senate will be reduced by fifty percent. Only half of our federal lawmakers will be around to foolishly spend our money. The enormous expenses of bribing them will be cut in half. The budget will be balanced because half of the fat retirement payments the politicians have voted for themselves won't have to be paid.

Like modern pharmaceutical products, the envisioned Population Reduction Program is not without its own side effects. If the scheme is successful, what with the huge influx of politicians, lawyers, used car salesmen and liberals, Hell may experience an overcrowding completely unforeseen by the devil. It may take eons for him to absorb them and the waiting line may be expected to be long, long, long. When we who remain on earth die, there may be no room for us in Hell. We may have to go to Heaven. That would be hell for those of us who can't stand singing or harp music.

Before putting the Population Reduction Program into effect, operational parameters must be established. We can't simply pass a law authorizing the killing of half the people in the country and let it go at that. If we go out and shoot everyone who deserves it, we'll reduce the country's population by more than 75 percent, substantially exceeding the bag limit. Some of us would be subject to rebuke and, given the current condition of our judicial system, we might even be fined! No, we must have rules.

The rules identifying those to be exterminated must be drafted with extreme caution and reflect careful judgment. Otherwise there could be some terrible miscalculation which could result in you or me (more especially me) being included in the list to be plowed under.

Given terminology avoiding the chance of such a tragedy, the Reduction List should not be otherwise discriminatory. By that I mean outdoorsmen should not be excluded automatically. We have all seen duck hunters who apparently believe they have deer rifles. Any hunter who fires at a duck flying more than one-and-a-half times the range of his shotgun should be killed on the spot.

The Reduction List should include anyone who eats woodcock. Although it may not be a heinous crime warranting the death penalty, as a matter of public policy, such killings are justified if only for the reason of wiping out the breeding stock and, thus, raising the average IQ of the rest of humanity.

No one will miss the people who float down trout streams in rubber life rafts or canoes, improving the pristine quality of their surroundings by tossing beer cans here and there. The ones who float in front of the fisherman, paddling through the hole he is working, and then turn and ask: "Any luck?" should be the first to go.

Well, you get the idea. Become a part of the Population Reduction Program to save the environment. Get some crayons and write to your Senator or Representative. Print in large block letters.

Prepare to Meet Thy Doom

It's kind of sad to see some wizened and decrepit guy being wheeled into a sport shop and watch him buy a new deer rifle. The old timer knows full well he'll never live until November. For years he's wanted a new deer rifle. Now he has it, but he's waited too long to get the chance to use it.

If he had known he had only eighteen months to go, he could have bought the gun last February and got one full season's use out of it. Now, the purchase serves no good purpose. No good purpose for him, that is. You might be able to buy it from his estate at half price.

Hunters are seldom preoccupied with their own demise. This is nothing more than a matter of priorities. Usually, they're too busy thinking about pheasant and grouse and dogs and ducks to be bothered with such unhealthy meditations. Ever since washing machines replaced scrub boards, hunters' wives have had a lot of free time on their hands and they are apt to use it by worrying about the terrible misfortune befalling them in the event their adored husband would pass away.

Last December, Daisy Cummins learned her second cousin's husband had died. He got hit by a car as he walked down a Wisconsin Avenue sidewalk in Milwaukee. The death came as a surprise to Daisy's now widowed second cousin because her husband failed to give any advance notice of the occurrence. In her letter to Daisy, the widow complained of her husband's careless oversight.

That evening, Daisy asked her hunter husband, if he

entertained any such plans for an early demise. Daisy wasn't entirely satisfied with Carl's brief negative response and she immediately began to show an inordinate interest in Carl's well being. She investigated the amount of insurance carried on his life and the status of premium payments. Her concern was so great she proposed he postpone the purchase of a case of 7 1/2 chilled shotgun shells in favor of the purchase of a new Whole Life Policy.

Then things got worse - much, much worse. Daisy read a newspaper account of a deer hunter who shot a buck and then dragged it out of the woods, only to have a fatal heart attack and die before a picture could be taken of him and the dead animal.

The Animal Rights people felt the picture of a hunter and a dead deer could be used as a gimmick to show the cruelty of hunters. Such a picture could be used in a direct mail fund raising effort and would surely bring in thousands of dollars from the weak minded. The Animal Rights lawyers immediately brought a suit for damages charging the hunter with negligence in dying before the picture could be taken. The jury brought in a multimillion dollar verdict and the estate went bankrupt.

Since Carl had refused to purchase any additional life or liability insurances, Daisy suggested the potential of his accidental death might be eliminated if Carl gave up hunting. She also told him she had arranged an appointment with a doctor where Carl would be subjected to all of the tests known to medical science in an effort to predict the year, month, date and time of day of his death.

And so, in early September, Carl visited Doc Carmichael. He carefully explained the background and reasons for the visit. Carl asked only two questions: What am I going to die of and when am I going to die? Carl thought a man should know those things. With absolutely no information concerning that coming event, a man might postpone a hunting trip until it was too late, just like the old timer buying the deer rifle.

Doc Carmichael knew Carl. He wouldn't even hazard a guess as to the how or the when of his demise. He allowed as how Carl might be shot tomorrow by some incensed business associate or outraged husband. He also recommended Carl get some exercise to preserve his physical condition for as long as possible and informed him that unless he took good care of himself he would never live long enough to earn the money needed to pay the substantial bill the Doc was going to charge for the check-up.

Doc Carmichael then wrote a report which he delivered to Carl who passed it on to an Egyptologist with a reputation for being able to translate obscure hieroglyphics. Then Carl showed the translation to Daisy. It said:

"The cholesterol and blood pressure levels are elevated and are of serious concern. The white cells seem confused and wander aimlessly throughout those things I think they call veins and arteries. Lungs show a disturbing increase in the presence of house dust and cat hair.

"Indication of psychological pressure at work and in the home appear to be factors contributing to the subject's general debilitated condition. Such stress could cause a fatality without notice.

"An exercise regimen is recommended. Week-end activity in the open air, far from an urban or sub-urban environment is essential. A walking program is advised. The swinging of arms or the carrying of extra weights is also recommended if full advantage of the walking program is to be obtained.

"Life threatening allergy to cat hair can be overcome by occasional antidotal association with dogs. Return for another examination in early December."

In accordance with the medico's advice and at the insistence of Daisy, on the following Saturday, which happened to be the opening day of the pheasant season, Carl was far from the madding crowd, walking in an open field. He was carrying an extra weight. It was a double barreled 12 gauge shotgun. As per the doctor's suggestion, he was also in association with a dog. It was a Brittany Spaniel named T-Bone.

T-Bone was three years old and was just coming into her own as a hunting dog. Its owner, Doc Carmichael, was also present in case emergency medical attentions were needed. Following his own advice, he, too, carried a shotgun.

For the balance of the fall season Carl and Doc Carmichael and T-Bone all enjoyed healthful week-end outdoor activity. After the end of the deer season, Carl and Daisy returned to the clinic for his scheduled examination. They received great news. The exercise regimen needed no longer to be followed - but stress had to be avoided. The doctor also recommended Carl's medical condition be reviewed during the first half of the following September.

Next year Doc Carmichael planned to prescribe the necessity of absolute silence in the home and the need for the occasional ingestion of medicinal dosages of Scotch whisky.

The King of Egypt

Farouk I was the last King of Egypt. A man of gourmand eating habits, the King was a very large fellow. He was also a trout fisherman. Though not reported by the historians, it was his custom to make an annual visit to Upper Michigan and northern Wisconsin for the purpose of pursuing the sport.

Because of his huge girth and substantial bulk, the King had difficulty wading in the small rocky streams. He would slip and slide and fall and fill his Octuple X Large sized waders with regularity.

I have often claimed I fished with Farouk and, in a manner of speaking, it is the truth. Actually, I was not a member of the King's party. I happened to be fishing upstream from him. I clearly remember it was a day of very strange fishing. There would be no action until suddenly the Brook trout would engage in an uninterrupted feeding. In a few minutes it would stop and then - nothing. Fifteen or twenty minutes later, the same feeding pattern would again occur.

During one of the periods of inactivity, I heard terrible splashing sounds coming from the stream below me. They frightened me. I thought it was a flock of bears. I was preparing to quickly return to the safety of my car, but the same excited feeding started. So I continued to fish. My fishing was interrupted when one of his majesty's bodyguards discovered my presence. I was forced to leave the area.

That evening, after giving the matter considerable thought, I believe I discovered the reason for the peculiar fishing I had experienced. Whenever King Farouk fell into the water, the sound of his splashing and the associated rise in the water level convinced the trout the world was coming to an end. Deciding they wanted to go on a full stomach, the fish swam upstream and gorged themselves on whatever food was available.

It tested my theory. A friend threw a huge stone into the water while I waited upstream. My guess was proven to be accurate. In less time that it takes to tell, I caught and released a limit of large Brook trout. In honor of the King, I christened that fishing system: "Farouking".

My trout fishing companions, without exception, will tell you I have "farouked" up more trout streams than anyone they know.

The Luckiest Man in the World

Jerry Olson went to Wyoming and shot an elk. He celebrated. He celebrated quite a bit. When he awoke the following afternoon, he found a receipt showing he had bought an American Bison - on the hoof. He also found another receipt showing he had shipped it home. If you think it's hard to get rid of old National Geographic magazines, think about trying to get rid of live bison.

Jerry solved his problem by donated the animal to the local D. U. Chapter for a raffle item at their annual banquet. He took a substantial charitable deduction in his income tax return and considered himself to be lucky, indeed.

Over eight hundred tickets were sold for the Live Buffalo Drawing. John Meyers bought one. So did Ron Tuttle. Each had exactly the same chance to win. For every person who is extraordinarily lucky, there is another person who is extraordinarily unlucky. It has to be that way. The statisticians insist upon it. John Meyers is lucky - very, very lucky. Ron Tuttle is not lucky - very, very not lucky.

As you have probably guessed, John Meyers did not win the buffalo. Ron Tuttle had that misfortune. The morning after the DU banquet, while John was enjoying a late sleep-in, Ron was trying to explain to his wife why a buffalo was tied up in the back yard. At the same time, he was trying to remember what he had been told about family support orders and property division in divorce matters and wondering if the judge would order him to pay his wife's attorney fees, too.

John Meyers has always enjoyed good fortune. For instance - last year when the leaves began to fall and his wife started her annual campaign to get him to take care of the yard before he disappeared into the Ruffed Grouse season, someone broke into John's garage and stole his rake. I'll tell you how lucky he is. Last spring the State's lottery prize had grown to over 8 million dollars. John needed money to finance a trip to Labrador for some Atlantic Salmon fishing. When I found out he had bought a ticket, I didn't buy one because I fully expected him to hold the winning number.

John is a trout fisherman - perhaps not a good one, but a very lucky one. It's his practice to keep his fishing license and a twenty dollar bill in a tightly closed plastic folder stuffed into the upper pocket of his fishing vest. This protects them from getting wet when unsuccessful mid-stream gymnastics are executed. It also keeps the license and the twenty dollar bill in proper condition should he meet a warden or be required to prove his age or come upon a tavern located at streamside.

It is also John's practice to smoke cigars while he fishes. He does this solely to protect his health and physical well being. The smoke discourages disease carrying mosquitoes and no-see-ums from attacking him. In addition, when a large trout takes a fancy to a fly and explodes from the water, unless he has a cigar in his mouth, a fisherman could easily break a tooth when he automatically and violently sets his jaw.

In preparation for the potential Labrador trip, John went to the Wolf River to practice casting in the pool below the Oxbow. When he pulled the cigar from his vest pocket, he didn't notice he also dislodged the little plastic folder. It dropped into the river and then he saw it floating away. Before he could attempt the retrieval, it had gone past a large rock and started through the flat water behind it.

As he watched it sail away, a Brown trout as big as your

leg came half way out of the water and easily swallowed the little plastic package. With his usual good luck, John had discovered one of the Oxbow's prime feeding stations and a trout so large and menacing that, upon seeing it, lesser men would have fled the river in terror. For the next two hours, John threw everything in his fly box over, around, and near that big rock and through that flat water below it, but he came up empty. He didn't even get a short hit and the huge Brown refused to rise again.

A few days later, when the winning lottery number was announced, John couldn't find his ticket. Then he remembered he had put it in that little plastic envelope together with the license and the twenty dollars. When the sun arose the following Saturday morning, the multimillion dollar prize had not yet been claimed and John was at the Oxbow. He carefully planned his attack. Stationing himself where he could get the right drift around the rock and into the flat water, he lit his cigar.

He then took a plastic folder from his pocket. It was the same size and shape of the one that had held his license, his twenty dollars and his lottery ticket. He attached it to a size 10 Mustad hook tied to an eight pound test leader. Then he flipped the package into the current. It drifted over the same spot where the big Brown had struck the week before. All hell broke loose.

When the huge trout was brought to net, John waded to the bank and then walked another fifteen feet into the woods, just to be sure the fish wouldn't get back into the water. He took the big Brown from the net, sliced the fish open and retrieved the same plastic folder it had swallowed a few days earlier - or at least what was left of it.

Though the plastic folder hadn't passed through the trout, it was so digested that neither the license nor the twenty dollar bill nor the lottery ticket were anywhere near being recognizable. In disgust John threw the offal and the remains of the package back into the river.

Lucky John. The Judge believed his story and (to the obvious dissatisfaction of the Warden and District Attorney) he dismissed the charges of Fishing Without a License, and Keeping a Trout in a Catch and Release area.

Where Did It Come From

Last January I was confined to the house because it was too cold and windy to go outside and ice fish. There wasn't much to do. In desperation, I picked up a book and wiled away the time by reading it. Its title was catchy - The American Heritage Dictionary of the English Language.

The cast of characters is very large. The first one it mentions is an old-time Greek named Achilles. Then, after scattering the names of all the presidents of the United States throughout the book, it ends up with a Persian prophet named Zoroaster. There were many, many other characters. I couldn't keep track of them all.

Unless you are suffering mightily from insomnia, I cannot recommend the book to you. It is boring, boring, boring. I couldn't get interested in it. As far as I was concerned, the American Heritage Dictionary has no plot of any kind and there is absolutely no continuity in the writing. If you get a chance to read it, don't.

It stayed cold and windy all day long and I remained house bound. With nothing else to do, I decided I could use the time to good advantage by being helpful to What's-Her-Name. I followed her around and made suggestions on how she could do the housework in a more efficient manner. I don't know how many times I told her "You missed a spot" when she was sweeping or scrubbing the kitchen floor.

Sometimes I don't understand that woman. She broke into my gun cabinet, took out my 38/55 Winchester rifle and loaded it. She said she was going to shoot me - just because I was being helpful.

Anyway, to be on the safe side, I barricaded myself in the den. Outside the door, What's-Her-Name was still raving. It took almost an hour for her to quiet down and even then, every so often I'd hear her sneak up to the den door and snarl. I thought it would be smart if I stayed put.

I got to thinking about that dictionary. I wondered where all those words came from. That was too broad a subject to comprehend so I narrowed it down and wondered about the source of our hunting and fishing terms. The origins of some of our special vocabulary are easy to determine. The Setter and the Pointer are examples. (Charlie Ainsworth had a dog he described as a kind of Setter and Pointer - an upsetter and a disappointer.)

Some words come from the imitation of a sound associated with the animal. The word "goose" does not fall into that category, but the word it comes from does. The ancient Indo-European word for "goose" was "ghans". The German "gans" and the Spanish "ganso" are still used in those countries. The next time you want to induce a flock of Canadas to fly over your decoys, try holding your nose (to produce the proper nasal sound), and, from the back of your throat, yell "ghans".

In the fifth and sixth centuries, Angles, Saxons and Jutes migrated to England. They spoke Germanic dialects which became what we now call "Old English". Their verb "doucan" meant to pull one's head down, suddenly. They saw a bird that did it and they called it a "doke". Now you know where "duck" came from. It describes both the bird and my action whenever What's-Her-Name reaches for a weapon.

In the Old English of the Anglo Saxon, the word "doer" meant "animal" and by that they meant any living creature which was not a human being. That covers a lot of territory. By the tenth century, the word had come to mean only the four legged creature we know as "deer".

The root of our word "bear" also lies in the Old English language. Their word "bera" came from the Germanic "bero", which meant "brown". Apparently there were no silver tip grizzlies running around prehistoric Germany.

When the Spanish Conquistadores came into Mexico in the 1500s, they discovered a strange new bird. They'd never seen anything like it. In Spain they had the peacock, which they called the "Pavo Royal". (A professor at the University got a government grant and, after a year of study, came up with the translation from Spanish into English. He called it a "Royal Pavo.") That strange new bird is now called "pavo" in most Spanish speaking countries, but in Mexico, it is called by the proper Nahuac Indian term "guajolote".

The New World English colonist also saw the bird and didn't know what it was. In their experience, the only bird which came close to it was the guinea fowl. The guinea fowl originated in Africa and found its way into Europe by way of Turkey. The Brits called the guinea fowl "Turkey Cock" (or "Turkey Hen" - I don't want the N.O.W. girls to get upset and accuse me of gender discrimination.) That's why we call it a "turkey".

The Europeans had trouble with the term to be used to identify the New World's moose. Spanish dictionaries translate "moose" as "alce". They also translate "elk" as "alce". Our word "moose" come from the language of the Algonquian and is translated as "one who eats bark".

Early Canadian settlers had another problem. They didn't know if the plural of moose was "mooses" or "meese" - as in the case of "goose/geese". They solved the problem by reporting to their hunting companions: "I saw a moose. In fact, I saw a herd of five of them."

The language of the Algonquian Indians forms the basis of many of our hunting and fishing words. They called a small dexterous animal by the name "arathcone". The word meant "one who scratches with his hands". We call it a raccoon. The Algonquian also came up with the word "maskinouge". Today it is pronounced "muskellunge".

They called another animal the "khalibu". Khalibu meant "one who paws". The French in Canada changed it to "caribou". The Spanish dictionary translates "caribou" as "reno". The reno is a reindeer, like the ones they have in Lapland. Europeans seem to have trouble getting things right.

The Hungarian Partridge has been assigned the Latin name of Perdix Perdix Perdix. The word "perdix" has a Greek root. It means an action which can be clearly described through the use of an uncouth four lettered Elizabethan term. The publisher of this book claims to be dedicated to family values. He also believes discretion is the better part of valor. He says I can use the phrase "breaking wind". If a Hun takes off unexpectedly from beneath your feet, perhaps it sounds something like that.

As everyone knows, the pheasant was named after the Rioni River. It flows westerly from the Caucasus Mountains and enters the Black Sea a bit north of Turkey. The River used to be called the Phases. The bird came from there and the old Greeks called it "phasianos" - "Phasian" bird. It's only a short step from there to "pheasant".

My investigations into hunting and fishing word origins was cut short when, three days later, it got warmer and the wind stopped blowing. By that time, What's-Her-Name had calmed down quite a bit. When she unlocked the den door from her side, I took a chance. I removed the barricade from my side and went ice fishing.

Friendship

Hunters and fishers, we all agree, are a class unto themselves. There is a strong bond between us. It goes unrecognized and unappreciated by the rest of the people who occupy lower classifications within the Homo sapiens genus. In the field and on the stream, hunters and fishermen may meet as strangers, but, after only a few minutes, they can form a friendship which, in some cases, lasts for hours.

Freddie Reinheimer is a case in point. Freddie is a grouse shooter-ater, a noted catch-and-release deer hunter and an avid trout fisherman. He is also a capable camp cook. He has prepared meals in various camps for well over twenty years and claims he never lost a man. He is, therefore, welcomed by and popular with those outdoorsmen who prefer to spend their time hunting or fishing rather than splitting wood, cooking and washing dishes.

Freddie is one of our very good friends. When in the field, he usually gets up before sunrise, starts the camp fire, gets the coffee going and prepares the breakfast menu. Sometimes he will pick fresh blueberries for the pancakes or, perhaps, black-berries for a side dish. At the appropriate time he will awaken his still sleeping companions and dish out the food.

When we have eaten and disappeared into the woods or down the stream, Freddie heats the water and washes the dishes. After this task has been accomplished, it is his custom to pick up the chain saw and gas can, get into the truck and drive a mile or two until he finds a dry hard wood deadfall.

He'll cut firewood for the wood stove, returns to camp and unload it. Then it will be time to begin the preparation of lunch since we will soon return from our morning hunting or fishing endeavors.

After the rest of the troops have enjoyed their mid-day lunch, Freddie tends the fire in the cabin wood stove, heats more water, washes more dishes and cleans any birds or fish we have brought back to camp. He polices the camp site, but won't split the fire wood collected in the morning. He doesn't want to disturb us because we are all enjoying a nap.

As soon as we are awake and have again disappeared to hunt or fish, Freddie will split enough wood to keep the campfire going long into the night. Freddie is efficient and usually finds time to spend an hour or so hunting or fishing after he has completed his preparations for the evening meal. All of us truly appreciate Freddie.

As I say, Freddie enjoys hunting and fishing with his friends. He knows we are his friends because we all compliment him on the quality of his meals and on the way he mixes the drinks. He is popular in camp and is always invited on our expeditions.

Last year Freddie decided to give us a spaghetti dinner. It doesn't take much time to cook spaghetti. All you do is dump it into boiling water, but the sauce - ah, that is a different matter. Freddie makes his sauce from scratch and it is the sauce that makes his spaghetti exceptional. The basic mushrooms, onions and tomatoes give the proper color and texture. The oregano and spices makes it good, but it is the special home-made sausage that makes Freddie's spaghetti sauce great.

Freddie provides us with an Italian style sausage made in a family operated meat market. It deserves all of the praise it is given. Its taste simply cannot be beaten. Freddie knows how to prepare it. He simmers a couple dozen of the links in the sauce for a full day. Then all he has to do is boil the water for the spaghetti and heat up that great sausage filled sauce.

Freddie began making the sauce in the afternoon. The sausages went in and the iron pot was pushed to the back of the wood stove where it slowly simmered. It was still warm the next morning. By noon it was almost ready. When the gang got back in the late afternoon, it wouldn't take much time to boil the water and heat the sauce.

After splitting the wood for the evening fire, Freddie had plenty of time to put on his waders, get his fly rod and splash out into the stream that bordered the cabin site. And this he did. The trout stream had a number of tributaries. A few hours later, on his way back to camp, Freddie went up the wrong one and got lost.

The rest of us had returned from a hard day of casting, netting and releasing. We were all exhausted and hardly had the strength to open the cooler chest and get the ice cubes for the restorative libations. An hour later, someone noticed there were no hors d'oeuvres on the table. Not only that, we had to add wood to the fire all by ourselves. Intending to chastise him for the oversights, we called out, but Freddie did not respond.

This was, indeed, an upsetting discovery. We sincerely feared the occurrence of a calamity. We had all counted on an evening meal. Our apprehensions were allayed when we found the spaghetti and the sauce readied for the final few minutes of preparation. One of the more experienced fishermen put the water on the stove and in no time it was merrily boiling away. The spaghetti was added and soon we were enjoying a hearty meal.

When the after dinner brandy and the cigars were distributed, our thoughts again returned to our absent companion. Not only was Freddie missing, but his waders and fly rod were not to be found. Apparently, he had gone fishing. He was either lost or had drowned. Again, a panic terror seized us. Who would prepare breakfast?

Tragedy was averted when, as the moon rose, a bedraggled and sweating Freddie crawled up the stream bank and into camp. After apologizing for the failure to prepare hors d'oeuvres, Freddie headed for the spaghetti. It was a cold, congealed lump. The remaining sauce looked like something the dog had thrown up. Freddie made a fuss because that cold sauce contained only two small pieces of his favored Italian sausage.

His complaints subsided when it was pointed out that had we not had the foresight to cut one of the sausage links in half, he would have had only one piece.

We all adopted a charitable attitude and forgave his outburst. After all, what are friends for?

Planked Chicken

As irrefutable proof of their bias and lack of balance, the ABC, NBC and CBS news programs don't give much attention to the merits of salt, pepper, thyme and rosemary. Oh, how quickly they forget. It was only four or five hundred years ago that herbs were the motivating force behind one helluva lot of activity.

It wasn't wanderlust that caused Marco Polo to head for China and it wasn't only fireworks he brought back with him. Columbus' financial backers weren't interested in discovering Salvador Island or Haiti. Vasco da Gama and Magellan took to the seas for the same reasons motivating Christopher Columbus. They all wanted to get to a place where they could load up with exotic spices, sail back home and sell them for a bundle.

After all, in those days the refrigerator had not yet been invented. Something had to be added to mask the taste of the pork chops that had been hanging in the back room during two weeks of August heat. If Cinnamon or Ginger or Allspice or Cayenne or Nutmeg weren't available, the Royal Taster was in for a very bad time of it and the Royal Cook was in danger of being separated from his head.

This was all very understandable. Suppose the only food you had to eat was a woodcock, Further suppose it had been a very warm September and the cabin had been out of ice for over a month. Finally, suppose there was a plant growing in a neighbor's back yard with leaves which, if picked, dried and shredded, would make woodcock taste good. (The possibility of there being a factual basis for that third assumption is about the same as the possibility of your real estate taxes being reduced. Nevertheless, let's all make believe there is such an herb.)

Question: Would you not kill for such a spice? Of course you would. Your life would depend upon it. Faced with the alternative of starving to death or eating a woodcock without that fabled plant's fabled leaves or, in the alternative, an amply supply of kerosene sauce or something equally able to hide its taste, no man with an IQ exceeding that of a garden slug would do other than starve.

Civilization has made some advances since the final days of the Dark Ages. Insulated ice chests will keep ice cubes available and food can be kept in gas refrigerators if there is no electricity at camp. Foodstuff need no longer turn green. Meat remains fresh and requires nothing special to make it palatable. (Except, of course, woodcock and nothing can make it palatable.)

This does not mean spices have no place in camp. Hunters, generally, have become accustomed to delicate flavorings, but camp cooks don't have to go to the Andaman Islands to get seasoning for the salad. If the camp cook runs out of mace for the oyster stew or realizes he has forgotten the marjoram for the soufflé, he can usually get into the truck and find a town within thirty miles of camp where he can buy the stuff.

If the cook is knowledgeable or has imagination, he may find something close to the camp that will give a special taste to the food he prepares. In the springtime, wild leek may be better than onion. A leek in the soup will give it a unique flavor. Bruised wintergreen is a great substitute for mint in any drink or recipe.

Many well organized camps have their own herb gardens

where parsley, sage, chives and basil are cultivated. With these and other condiments on hand, the camp cook may create an impromptu mixture of seasonings which, like the lost chord, can never be reproduced. Such was the case with Smokey Armstrong and his now famous recipe for planked chicken.

Over the years, Smokey developed a reputation for being a messy cook. It seemed to come naturally to him. When he was in the camp kitchen he was awkward and disorderly. He had a penchant for knocking things over. Chaos and disarray were his constant companions. The kindest way to describe his kitchen was to call it a disaster area.

During deer season when he was out of the cabin and on a deer stand, Smokey developed a reputation for being a messy hunter. He wiggled. He squirmed, He coughed. He noisily unwrapped candy bars and smoked smelly cigars. While on drives, he usually had his eyes glued to the ground in front of him and missed seeing the deer that were running around him. When his eyes weren't glued to the ground, he'd get his feet tangled and fall down a lot, making enough racket to frighten deer from beds three ridges beyond the horizon.

In fourteen years, Smokey (a) never shot a deer, and, (b) never shot at a deer. Thereafter, he very seldom left the cabin to join his fellow hunters on stands or in drives. Nevertheless, he was very popular in camp. He was a passable (though untidy) cook and he had never left the poker table a winner.

Smokey wasn't given to strong drink so I was surprised when I returned to camp in mid-afternoon and found him at the woodstove holding a half empty bottle of brandy. That bottle had not been opened at noon when the rest of us returned from our stands for Smokey's noon-time lunch of soup and Baloney Sandwiches. (There's a lot of soup and B S served up in deer camp when the hunters come in for their lunches.)

When I got back to camp that afternoon, Smokey had been

preparing to roast a chicken for dinner. He was smiling and singing and scattering sage, poultry seasoning, flour, brandy and other spices. Some of it had found its way on and into the chicken. Lots of it was heaped up in small piles on the counter. An equal amount had found its way to the cabin floor. There was a reason for all his merriment.

When he realized I had entered the cabin a few hours earlier than usual, Smokey greeted me, took a sip from the bottle and, using a butcher knife as a pointer, he motion toward the deer pole. Through the window I could see a six point buck hanging from it. Smokey told me he had been dozing in an easy chair when he looked up and saw a buck walking across the cabin yard.

Smokey had shot his first deer. He gutted it, managed to pull it up on the deer pole and, understandably, began celebrating. He had been celebrating for some time when I entered the cabin.

Now friends, I didn't think it was healthy for Smokey to drink all that brandy. So I helped him. It seemed like the sociable thing to do - first buck and all that. We had a convivial time of it. As the day wore on, the celebration may have verged on the boisterous. Anyway, we had a happy though jumbled and messy afternoon.

The kitchen may have looked like the Vandals had landed and sacked the place, but the chicken sure smelled good. The sun was down when the rest of the crew returned from the woods. By that time Smokey's Planked Chicken was done and it was superb.

Unfortunately, Smokey couldn't quite recall exactly what he had done to the chicken. I had watched him as he prepared the bird, but I hadn't actually helped with the seasoning so I can't be faulted for not remembering the precise quantities or kind of herbs he used. In the years that have passed, I've become a deer camp cook and more than once I've tried to reproduce Smokey's Planked Chicken.

Each year I carefully measure differing quantities of Maple leaves, melted snow, wood ashes, pine needles and all the spices I recall Smokey having spilled on the boards which form the floor of the kitchen area. I throw them all on the planking, just like Smokey did nine years ago. Then I drop a half baked chicken on it, just like Smokey did nine years ago. I kick the bird around four or five times, just like Smokey did when he tried to pick it up. Then I brush it off and put it back in the oven for another couple of hours.

But I've never been able to recreate that special flavor of Smokey's Planked Chicken.

Canard Violans

Dave Anderson was a standard, garden variety duck hunter. By that I mean he'd be in a marsh or a duck boat for 90 percent of the time when duck hunting was legal. The other ten percent of the time he would be near a marsh or a duck boat watching an in-progress gale or home nursing a bad cold or a case of frostbite incurred while he was in or near a marsh or duck boat.

You will, therefore, understand that Dave wasn't a fanatic duck hunter. He displayed only the usual interests and actions of other normal, garden variety duck hunters. He behaved as rationally as you or I might behave during the duck hunting season.

One day last spring, Dave was walking out of a Minnesota evening establishment after spending an hour or so in the negotiation of agreements for the purchase and sale of glasses of water diluted with Scottish drinking whisky. As he approached the door, he passed a group of 20 years-olds. "You guys can say what you want," one of them argued, "but for my money, you can't beat a Redhead."

Dave was immediately filled with a sense of gratification. He rejoiced in the knowledge that the younger generation was showing such obvious signs of mature judgment. It was a pleasure, indeed, to see young men sitting in a tavern and discussing duck hunting.

Dave had never considered the Redhead to be a duck with any special or even noteworthy characteristics. It didn't have the cautious cunning of a Canvasback or a Sprig. It was just a duck ... or was it? Dave got to thinking about all this and decided he might be missing something. So, he embarked on an in-depth study of the Redhead. He dug out a 1966 edition of the New Hunter's Encyclopedia and learned the duck had the fancy Latin name of Canard Violans.

Among other gems of information, he learned lady Canard Violans were apt to lay their eggs in the nest of other ducks. She didn't give a tinker's dam if it was the nest of a Canvasback, a Ruddy Duck or whatever. That explains why it is not uncommon to find Redheads in the migratory flights of Canvasback. It may also explain the marital strife and high divorce rates within the Ruddy Duck community where drakes often accuse hens of all kinds of infidelities.

In studying the Canard Violans private lives, Dave discovered the hen is sometimes the aggressor if courtship occurs on the surface of a lake or pond. However, when the ducks are engaged in aerial courtship, the role of pursuer is always taken by the drake.

(For your information, the honey bee mates only while flying very high above the earth. This explains why the artificial insemination of the honey bee is so very seldom accomplished. I thought you'd like to know that.)

In his studies, Dave also discovered the Canard Violans is a gregarious creature that can be attracted by special types of decoy layouts. Dave had never paid much attention to the specific kind of decoy sets especially designed to induce the Redhead to land within it. He became curious and embarked on a study of Redhead sets.

Dave created his own decoy layouts calculated to attract passing Redheads. They worked. Dave became a successful Redhead hunter. Toward the end of the season when the diving ducks came down from Canada, Dave would hunt on Mille Lacs Lake and if the Canard Violans were in the area, his sets would bring them in and he would get more than his fair share of them.

Dave's reputation as a Canard Violans hunter became widely recognized. He decided to share his decoying secrets with fellow duck hunters - for a price. He wrote a pamphlet and placed the following ad in a number of magazines:

"Want To Attract Redheads? Send me $10 for a sure fire method."

Thousands of young men responded and Dave was soon busy running to the post office, mailing out the pamphlet describing his decoy sets, picking up the new mail and running to the bank to make deposits.

Some people just can't stand to see the free enterprise system succeed. It didn't take long before the authorities were after Dave. Malcontents mailed an avalanche of complaints to the U. S. Postal Service, to the Better Business Bureaus and to the Federal and State Attorney General Offices. They whined about being misled and claimed the mails were being used to defraud them.

The Postal Inspector happened to be a duck hunter. He recognized the true value of the set designs and dropped all charges against Dave. He did, however, insist Dave change the first line of his advertisements to read:

"Want To Attract the Canard Violans?" instead of "Want To Attract Redheads?"

After that, Dave's mail order business went to hell in a hurry. Young men stopped sending him money. Undaunted, Dave tried another approach. He decided to market through television. He produced an entire series of programs dedicated to the Canard Violans and his special decoy sets.

You can imagine his disappointment when the Minneapolis television stations refused to air his show. When Dave insisted he be given the reason for the refusal, the Station Manager explained there already was too much Sets and Violans on television.

The Doldrums

Sometime around the autumnal equinox when day light and darkness are the same length, the Government says: "You can't fish trout anymore this year." The Supreme Court has yet to decide if such a decree violates our constitutional right of due process, but it makes life tough for some of us. Certainly, it is the beginning of a period when life is not all beer and skittles for the trout fishermen.

Bears and opossums hibernate. The Homo sapiens isn't so fortunate. He has to face up to eight months, more or less fully conscious and without a fly rod in his hand. Many fishermen become dejected and gloomy and listless and seem to be indifferent to life itself. Medicos refer to it as "Trout Fisherman's Depression".

In an effort to keep them from giving up completely and voluntarily surrendering to the morticians, the Society To Protect Trout Fishermen From Becoming An Endangered Species was established. Due to a printer's error in our fund raising letters, the word "Fisherman" somehow or other dropped out of our Society's name and we received handsome grants from the federal government and from both the environmental group warning against the dangers of global warming and the one warning against the dangers of global cooling.

Once the grant monies had been received, the members of our Society met at three different Argentine lodges nestled next to the Andes and near the Traful, the Chimehuin and the Colon Cura Rivers where the trout season was open and where

Browns and Brooks and Rainbows abound.

When all grant money was spent, the four of us returned to the United States. Luckily we had drawn a list of activities designed to distract the trout fisherman from his morbid questioning of whether life was worthwhile when the trout streams were off limits. The results of the Society's deliberations are here published for the first time.

IN THE FALL - The trout fisherman can busy himself with the jobs that should have been completed during the months when trouting was legal. That kind of job can no longer be avoided with such patent excuses as: "I hear there are a lot of speckled trout in Mill Creek."

So, the grass can now be cut. It has grown quite high during the spring and summer. It will keep you busy for at least a few days - whacking it down to size and then mowing it. The neighbors and the Weed Commissioner will be happier and, with any luck, the grass won't grow more than four or five inches before the first killing frost, thus obviating the necessity of having to repeat the procedure.

There are other autumnal activities to distract the trout fisherman from his melancholia. Windows are great when it comes to looking through walls, but if one is to insist upon such a luxury, there is a good deal of maintenance work involved. Personally, I've always considered the attentions paid to storm windows to be a tad ridiculous. Only a few weeks after I finally get around to taking them down during the last weeks of September, What's-Her-Name has to put them back up in preparation for the coming winter.

Raking the leaves can be wonderful fun. Working in the crisp, invigorating autumn air brings enjoyment to all of the senses - the sight of geese flying overhead in their southbound V formations - listening to the rustle of the leaves and enjoying their fantastic colorations. It's really a privilege to clean them from the gutters and rake them off the lawn. (This is what I tell the kid who lives next door. He's getting older and is becoming smarter and harder to convince. I nearly always end up paying him a buck an hour to do the job.)

IN THE WINTER - The time has come to make sure your fishing equipment will be ready for the opening day of next year's season. Now you have time to (a) locate the leak in the waders that has soaked your left leg every time you got into a trout stream; (b) tie flies; (c) try to remove the melted chocolate and the wet cigar stain from you fishing vest; (d) tie flies; (e) take the tapered fly line from your reel and reverse it - unless you already did it last year. In that case, buy a new fly line; and, (f) tie flies.

When all equipment has been appropriately readied, it must be put in a place where it will all be easily accessible when the government gives its mid-May announcement opening the trout season. For no apparent reason, wives sometimes object to rod, reels, waders and the other essential accoutrements being stored on the dining room table. Good husbands will overlook such strange behaviors in their mates. They should be secure in the knowledge that given enough time - twenty of thirty years - wives might get used to it.

The trout fisherman's hip flask must be reconditioned. Reconditioning consists of three steps. First, the Scotch whiskey left in the flask must be removed. Since the pseudo-ecologists consider it to be a crime against the peace and dignity of the United States to pour noxious substances into the sink or onto the ground, the prudent fisherman will avoid getting into trouble with the Environmental Protection Agency. He will drink the bit of Scotch remaining in his flask.

The second step consists of sterilizing the flask. Since whiskey is known to kill germs, pour some more of it into the flask and slosh it around. (To remove that whiskey from the flask, see the First Step, above.) Many trout fishermen believe it is best to repeat Step Two a few times in order to make sure the flask has been completely sterilized.

Finally, the flask must be re-filled - perhaps a few times.

IN THE EARLY SPRING enough snow has melted to allow you to get to your cabin. The time has come to swamp it down and clean it up. The first job is that of fly disposal. During your absence, when the mercury in the thermometer began to move toward the bottom of the bulb and it got colder outside, all the flies within forty acres began to move to the inside of your cabin. After the chief fly's annual report is made to the assemblage, the meeting is adjourned and the flies all crawl into cracks in the wall or fall to the floor and lie there on their backs.

They're everywhere, but they aren't dead. They're waiting for you to heat up the place during your springtime clean up. Then they'll all de-hibernate and buzz around in a raucous manner, scaring the mice, falling into your beer and committing other such outrages. I suppose you could kill them off with chemicals. The trouble is the poisons might get into the soufflé and polish you off too. There's a better way to handle the problem

When you return to the cabin for the first time, before you start a fire in the wood stove, sweep the flies up and toss them out the door. Last year they must have held a regional meeting in my shack. In April, I filled two dustpans with their inert bodies - not enough for a good meal, but, still, one helluva lot of flies.

Some women seem to obsess about insignificant matters. If your wife has been continually complaining about the things stored on the dining room table, get on her better side by investing in a bag of bird seed. She's sure to be favorably impressed by your sensitive interest in the birdies that fly around your cabin. Do not tell her the pine squirrels and the mice will get almost all of it.

If you have engaged in all of the between-trout-season activities recommended by the Society and glance at the calendar only to discover mid-May has not yet arrived, you will be left with the necessity of surviving the next few dry, stale and empty weeks. I suppose you could commit ice fishing. I suppose you could tie flies. It will be tough. Hang in there. Don't become discouraged. The opening of the trout season will be just around the corner.

Elementary, My Dear Watson

The body was found at the entrance of 22-1 Baker Street with only the hilt of a Malay kriss protruding from its back. Sherlock Holmes and Doctor Watson had examined the cadaver before the Inspector from Scotland Yard ordered its removal to the morgue for the further attentions of the Coroner. Now the two men returned to the rooms Holmes rented on the second floor of the building.

"I can say without fear of contradiction", Holmes said to Watson, "the man is left-handed and an upland game hunter. He owned a double barreled shotgun and wore shooting gloves."

"Amazing", said Dr. Watson. "How did you deduce all of that, Holmes? Hah! I'll wager it came from the fact of there being scratches around the wrist of the man's right hand.

"Hmmn" said Holmes as he settled into the overstuffed chair in his living area.

"Yes," continued Watson, "the scratches on his right wrist would mean he was warding off the branches with that hand as he walked through brushy country - carrying his shotgun in his favoured left hand. This suggests not only was he left-handed, but he was a hunter of the woodcock or the Ruffed Grouse that habituate that kind of woodland."

"Perhaps," said Holmes as he lit his calabash pipe.

"If he were left-handed," said Watson after a moment of reflection, "he probably used a double barreled shotgun because automatics and pump guns throw their empty casings in an inconvenient and disruptive manner for southpaw hunters."

Holmes nodded thoughtfully.

"Finally," Watson said, smiling and triumphantly concluding his analysis, "since he had scratches only on his wrist, he was, undoubtedly, wearing shooting gloves which protected the back and upper parts of his hand, but the lower portion remained exposed to the tearing of the brambles as he pressed through the upland bird covert."

He smiled at Holmes and asked, "Does that chain of logic represent the reasoning you followed in arriving at your deductions?"

"No," Sherlock Holmes replied. "I spent last Saturday afternoon hunting with him."

The Modern Trapper

The trapper was a very important figure in the history of the United States. A hundred years ago, meat produced by snares and traps helped the early settlers feed their families. Buckskin clothed them and pelts provided them with something to trade for gunpowder, salt and the other necessities of frontier living. Trapping made it possible for them to survive and start the process of turning the wilderness into civilization. Apparently there was no trapping in Arkansas, Massachusetts or New York City.

The trapper's importance to the development of modern life is too often overlooked or understated. He was the mountain man who first explored the West. It was his experience and his reports which led to the Louisiana Purchase, Lewis and Clark's Voyage of Discovery and the expansion of our then young nation. He provided the beaver skins from whence came the soft fur needed to produce the hats worn by all men who could afford them. He was the cornerstone of the empire of John Jacob Astor, the founder of the American Fur Company. He made Astor the richest man in the United States

It was the trapper who provided the hides of the mink and the fox, the otter and the beaver, the rabbit and the muskrat that made the coats which continue to be prized by those of the female persuasion - including many who weep at the thought of the Canadian seal harvests. It was the trapper who provided game for the tables of the best urban restaurants.

Nowadays, few people eat raccoon, skunk, beaver or

muskrat and the demand for supplies of such victuals is limited to such an extent that their sale will not even provide beer money for a trapper. What with the advent of the pseudo-environmentalists and their screams of anguish at the thought of the death of a muskrat, trapping has been discouraged. Few women buy natural fur coats and the market has gone to hell.

With all of those factors affecting the profession, the trapper is rapidly disappearing from the scene. In many of the environmentalist's lists, he is named as an endangered species. There is evidence to support that classification. Only the disappearance of the classic trapper can explain the explosions of the beaver population with the predictable result of the ruination of many a stretch of good trout water. Certainly there are fewer practitioners of the art than there used to be. On the optimistic side of the ledger, however, a new and younger group of trappers is in emergence.

As men and women regain their sanity and either permanently escape from places like Chicago and Philadelphia or simply buy recreational lands in the north woods, they discard the anti-trapping bias engendered by the propagandas of the fund raising groups that use all the monies they collect for administrative expenses (i.e. big salaries) or educational services (i.e. printing anti-outdoorsman literature for the purpose of raising even more money for administrative expenses - i.e. big salaries).

The renaissance in the trapping occupation has been created by a single class of these urban escapees. A moment's thought will identify that breed of individual. It is well established that women, throughout the ages, have been the most experienced and proficient of trappers. The number of marriage licenses issued each year shows they have lost none of their innate ability to ensnare. This is why, once they get into a woodsy setting, women become skillful trappers.

In the city, animal rights activism may fairly ooze from their pores, but once they see a mouse run across the cabin floor, women can't help themselves. They are quickly overcome by their primal urge to trap and kill. Left to his own devices, modern man would probably hunt and fish and live in peace with the mice, sharing his food and cabin with them. The female of the species is made of sterner stuff. Her urge to destroy the "wee, sleekit, cow'rin', tim'rous beasties" is overwhelming.

Show me a woman and a cabin full of mice and I'll show you a woman who will soon be running a trap line. Beverly Rosenow is a good example. She and her husband, Tom, have a cabin north of highway 70 in Forest County. The cabin has mice.

Bev first suspected the presence of mice when, one morning, she made pancakes out of what she thought was buckwheat flour. Tom told her they had only white flour in the cabin. She asked him what all those black specks were if it wasn't buckwheat flour. Tom told her and, true to her primordial female instincts, Bev went into the mouse trapping business.

After researching the matter, Bev invested in a half dozen mouse traps. Though she had no previous experience, she quickly became an expert. She soon became adept at setting mouse traps without having them go off prematurely and break a nail.

First, she considered the bait to be used. Women have millennia of experience in the selection and presentation of attractive baits. Eye shadow, lipstick, rouge and padded bras are examples of the lures they have employed to successfully entrap their prey.

Bev noticed Grey Squirrels loved the sunflower seeds she put on her bird feeder. She figured mice would like the same stuff. So, she coated the seeds with peanut butter and stuck them to the mouse traps' triggers. She ran her trap line under the sink and along the edge of the cabin's walls.

Then, using her feminine wiles, she dropped some seeds into a five gallon plastic pail, set it in the middle of the room and made a ramp by leaning a cedar stick from the floor to the top of the pail. When she and Tom returned the next weekend, they found three dead mice in the traps and three live mice in the bottom of the pail. The mice had crawled up the stick and jumped into the pail for the seeds, but they were unable to jump back out of it.

The task of mouse disposal was delegated to Tom. He performed that function quickly and quietly and secretly. Bev is completely unaware of what he does with them. If she can trap 503 more mice in that pail, Tom will have enough to be able to give her the fur coat she has wanted for all these years.

Bragging Rights

When you hear someone say: "Nobody likes a braggart", don't you believe him. The logic of that statement is faulty. If nobody liked a braggart, then nobody would brag. The simple fact of the matter is: Every one likes a braggart - if that "everyone" is the one doing the bragging.

There is a difference between bragging and lying. A fisherman can tell of the 24 inch brook trout that snapped his eight pound leader. If he has no witness, he will automatically be called a liar. If he has a picture of the fish, he will be called a braggart by everyone who has to listen to him.

It should be noted that any braggart who catches a 24 inch trout will always have at least one picture of it on his person. If that man is awakened in the middle of the night, a photo will immediately be produced from under the pillow and he will begin to tell you how he caught it.

The people who must listen to him feel uncomfortable and wish he would go away. He won't go away. He enjoys telling the story and bragging about his fishing expertise. He enjoys watching the discomfort of the others who must listen to his bragging. His bragging will not cease and his friends, his casual acquaintances, his enemies and the strangers he meets on the street will all have to put up with it.

By tradition, so old the memory of man runneth not to the contrary, the development of newer bragging rights terminates those of the person previously enthroned. When someone catches a bigger trout and can produce a photo, the displaced braggart will be automatically removed from Alpha Male status and relegated to the lower position of one who can only affect a look of disdain, call the new braggart "a braggart" and wish he would go away.

This is the reason outdoorsmen spend so much time hunting and fishing. They would rather be watching the Packer game, but they have to catch a bigger walleye or shoot a bigger turkey just to shut up the resident braggart. Then they will be able to take his place and watch their companions squirm as they recount the what, the where and the when of it - over and over and over again.

The hunter who gets the first buck in deer camp is recognized as having bragging rights, but only until someone gets a bigger one, and therein lies the tale.

George Peters had some trouble with his legs and couldn't run through the woods like a frightened fox. That's the sort of thing that might discourage a man from active participation in the deer hunt, but George was not easily discouraged. The DNR gave him a license to shoot from an automobile and George continued to hunt out of Doc Petersen's camp.

Doc built a road to the top of a hill overlooking a clear-cut area bordered by a swamp and every season George would drive to the top of that hill, position his car so he could cover what he considered to be the most likely area. Seated inside the vehicle, free from wind, snow and rain, George would wait for a buck to appear and hope he could roll down the car window in time to get a shot.

For years George had little opportunity to claim hunting prowess. "This morning, I saw twenty-six chickadees" or "Four deer came out of the swamp, but they didn't get to the spot where I could shoot at them" - those aren't the kinds of occurrences that give a man creditable bragging rights.

Doc's camp does cooperative hunting. If a buck manages to

run into a bullet fired by one of the hunters, the hunter is expected not only to share his meat with the others, but also to continue to hunt until all tags are filled. There are a lot of deer trespassing on Doc Petersen's property. His hunting friends usually have good luck and often fill up. Even when they do so, they don't make a dent in the size of he local herd.

Last year Doc invited his friend Ralph to join the hunt. Ralph never hunted anything in his life. He never fired a deer rifle and didn't even bring one into camp. It was universally acknowledged that he would get lost the very moment he was turned loose in the woods. He couldn't cook. If given an axe and told to split the wood, he would clearly be a danger to himself and to all others in the near vicinity.

Admittedly, Ralph was neither a hunter type nor a good "camp man". He did, however, have some good qualities. He was a likeable cuss. He told a good story and he usually lost at the poker table. In addition to these admirable characteristics, Ralph had an even more attractive quality. As a condition for being allowed to join Doc's camp, he had to buy a deer license. Ralph represented one more deer tag for Doc's gang to fill. Of course, that was the real reason he had been invited into camp.

Ralph didn't feel comfortable staying in camp alone when the rest of the men went out on the hunt. So, after replenishing the wood supply and washing the breakfast dishes on opening day, he and George got into the car and they drove up the hill to George's stand. During the next hour, George took advantage of Ralph's inexperience and regaled him with stories of woodsy lore. Ralph learned a lot - most of it false. He was told various and sundry stories of George's experiences as a deer hunter. They were unsupported by photos and, thus, mostly lies.

George was telling Ralph how the male porcupine usually bleeds to death after mating when he looked up and saw a big eight pointer stroll out of the swamp and walk to a place where George could get a good shot at it. When the smoke cleared, the buck was down in its tracks.

George handed his hunting knife to Ralph and gave him instructions on how to tag the deer. While still inside the car explaining how Ralph should tie the paper tag through the deer's hind foot, another eight pointer came out of the swamp, stood broadside and gave George another good shot. Ralph got the job of tagging both of them

Ralph managed to pull them to the car. With George giving him instructions, Ralph cleaned them, tied them to the trailer hitch and dragged them back into camp. Together they hung them from the deer pole. It was the first morning of the opening day and George had killed two big bucks. There was substantial reason for celebration. He and Ralph toasted the successful hunt - more than once.

For years George had to listen to a lot of bragging and now he could get revenge. He planned to exercise his bragging rights and he intended to be insufferable. His companions would have to listen to him tell and re-tell, in excruciating detail, the specifics of his kills. He would keep it up for the rest of the deer season - and probably for a good part of the next year's hunt too. However, the fates were unkind.

Around noon, Doc Petersen and the rest of the gang came in for lunch. They saw sixteen points of buck hanging from the deer pole and knew George's bragging would extend long into the night. Ralph and George came out of the cabin. Before George could claim his bragging rights, Ralph said: "You know, George, I believe my buck is bigger than yours.

The Old Ones Are the Best Ones

A few hunters were sitting around a pot bellied stove which was only a bit older than any one of them. It was the Thursday night before the Saturday morning opening of the deer season. So there was some Scotch, bourbon, sour mash, brandy and dry sherry present. If it had been Friday evening, the presence of those libations would not have been discernable because the camp rule dictated No Drinking on the evening before the opening of the season. But it was Thursday so an occasional nibble at the jug was acceptable behavior.

Now I don't mean to suggest any of the five were anything close to what even a WCTUer would call a boozer. They were all quite temperate. The fact that five different kinds of beverage have been identified means the five did not agree on many things and each had firm beliefs concerning the relative merits of attitude adjustment liquids.

The five had hunted together for many years. If you excluded the youngster (62 years old), the other four had shared that November camp for over thirty five years. Just because they didn't always agree does not mean this was an unhappy deer camp. It was a very happy camp. It was a delight to be there.

Though the phrase: "You're filled with fecal material" (or something like that) commonly rang out during the post dinner conversations, the bonds of friendship were never broken. They weren't even strained. Packer and Bear fans coexisted and discussed the relative merits of the two teams in calm and peaceful quiet (except for a more than occasional shout of "You're filled with fecal material").

These old timers had a secret. They liked each other. It is the younger hunters who more often get their noses out of joint and screw up a deer camp. Don't get me wrong. I'm not against younger hunters. All hunters are good people, but some are better than others. I happen to believe the old ones are the best ones. They tend to be a bit mellower.

For one thing, they've been in a lot of hunting camps and during the many years of wandering about in the out-of-doors, they've witnessed more than one strange happening. Their longer exposure to life has given them a wide variety of experiences and its fun to sit back and listen to them.

Emery had just finished telling how he acquired the bear skin which had hung on the cabin wall since sometime before the 1970s. Nobody remembered the exact date. Emery told the story once during every one of the subsequent deer seasons. It was an old story, but Emery enjoyed telling it and we all enjoyed listening to it. The old ones are the best ones.

There was a pause in the conversation and someone said: "Too bad about that deer hunter down at Gresham last year."

"Was there some trouble?"

"I don't believe I heard about it."

"What happened?"

"You must have seen it. It was in all of the papers."

"Not all of us get the Shawano Evening Leader, Floyd. What happened?"

"Well, this diplomat - I believe he was a member of the Czechoslovakian Consulate in Chicago - was a consummate deer hunter. According to the story, he had hunted with a group out of Gresham for five or six years and, supposedly, knew his way around the woods.

"Apparently he and his camp mates formed a very close

knit group. It was like this camp. Everyone looked out for everyone else. Remember the cold snap at the end of last year's season? It must have gotten down to ten below. They tell me the wind chill factor was down to thirty below. No civilized person would hunt in such teeth shattering conditions, but that Czech Consular official put on his flame orange and walked out to his stand. Like I say, he was a consummate deer hunter.

"During the evening meal, at about seven o'clock when the meat was all gone, someone noticed an empty chair at the table. After discussion, it was decided the Consular official was the one who was missing. By ten o'clock some of his camp mates thought he might have been lost.

"They drove a few of the roads around their hunting territory and blew the horn, but heard no response - possibly because the windows in the car were rolled up in order to keep the occupants toasty warm. It was still well below zero outside - a temperature they considered to be far too cold for an on-foot search of the area.

"The following morning the thermometer had climbed to a more pleasant 25 degrees and the wind stopped blowing. As soon as the breakfast was finished, a search team was organized. The starting point of their search was the Czech's usual deer stand. When the hunters got there, a scene of bloody gore assaulted their eyes.

"They found his deer rifle. It was empty of shells and its stock had been broken - as if it had been used as a club. Bits of flesh and blood soaked clothing and one fang marked and lacerated boot lay nearby. The paw prints of two bears were discovered. The disturbed red snow gave evidence of the terrible fight that must have occurred. Of course, the hunters tracked down the two animals and dispatched them both.

"Feeling they should give him a decent burial, his camp mates slit open the sow and searched her stomach contents for his remains. Not a trace of the man was found. Then they turned their attentions to the other beast and, sure enough, the Czech was in the male."

Like I say, the old ones are the best ones.

The Medical Profession

A hundred or so years ago, the state of their art was such that medical students had to steal bodies from graveyards in order to find out what our innards looked like. Today doctors are busy splicing genes, providing scenarios for television soap operas and performing all sorts of intricate carpentry on us. That's good progress by anyone's standard.

Nevertheless, I've heard a lot of hunters and fishermen complaining about them. The indictments commonly state: Medical Science may be all right if you intend to spend the rest of your life in a nursing home or in some other urban setting, close to a clinic which is dedicated to performing any and all services for which payment is guaranteed by the government and/or by the insurance companies. But what about those of us who want to get away from the carbon monoxide and chemically treated water belt?

A physician can't afford to pay his education debts and die a multi-millionaire if he lives in some small town where the nearest government approved hospital is a fifty miles away. A medico won't live in such a place and he certainly won't make house calls to cabins in the woods. Modern day medicine and modern day doctors have turned their backs on the hunter and the fisherman.

The age of non-invasive laser surgeries, MRIs, CAT scans and complicated radiation zapping machinery won't help you a bit if you become ill in camp. There will be no doctor hurrying to your side to apply leeches or bleed you. You will be on your own. I suppose you could use your mobile phone to call a medico, but it won't help you.

After dialing the number and selecting an appropriate language, you'll get a series of pre-recorded instructions of Byzantine complexity. By following instructions and punching 9 or 10 buttons, you will be led through a maze of alternatives. Then you'll finally arrive at your destination and hear another recorded voice telling you to take two aspirins and call back in the morning.

If you get sick in camp, you will have to learn to handle sickness and disease without reliance upon formalized medical attention. You may have to depend on folk medicine. There are those who believe reliance on folk medicine is grounds for the appointment of a Guardian. Still others recommend folk medicine and are absolutely convinced of its beneficial effects on mankind.

That second group believes the people who indiscriminately use folk medicine remedies will quickly die off and remove the breeding stock of the world's too-large a population of idiots. Thus, they claim reliance on folk medicine will have the beneficial effect of raising the average IQ of the rest of mankind.

A third group, however, think there is a lot to be said about traditional remedies

I won't peremptorily dismiss all home remedies as being entirely useless. For example, the Foxfire Books contains a unique remedy for the treatment of poisonous bites. On page 240 of Volume I, it is reported:

"If bitten by a Black Widow spider, drink liquor heavily from 3 p.m. to 7 p.m. You won't get drunk, you'll be healed."

Don't snicker. It works. I have a friend whose wife is a firm believer in the efficacy of folk medicine. Her husband, the poor fellow, reports being bitten by Black Widow spiders two or three times a week. His good wife insists he follow the Foxfire Book remedy. She is always overjoyed when he survives those repeated bites. However, he does get drunk. He must have some peculiar metabolic reaction to the spider's venom.

A lot of folk medicine recognizes the therapeutic value of booze. A cookbook published in 1879 (Housekeeping in Old Virginia) contains a treasury of home remedy prescriptions developed in early America. A medicine guaranteed to cure jaundice appears on page 491 - to-wit:

"Fill a quart bottle a third full of chipped inner cherry bark. Add a large teaspoonful of soda and fill the bottle with whiskey or brandy. Take as large a dose three times a day as the system will tolerate. If it affects the head un-pleasantly, lessen the quantity of bark."

Our forefathers sure knew how to cure jaundice. Makes you proud to be an American, doesn't it. It also makes you wonder why jaundice isn't as popular as it once was.

Students of folk medicine tell us Mayapple root, when dried and pounded, will cure constipation. Like faith, they say it is able to move mountains. Medicinal historians also report the inside of a banana skin or the juice from a green tomato is an effective treatment for poison ivy.

The Mayapple nostrum is of questionable value. When wandering around in the woods with an improperly functioning exhaust pipe, few of us have either the time or the inclination to look for the roots, dry them and then pulverize them. As far as the proposed treatment for poison ivy is concerned, usually we don't carry a banana with us and I can't get crabgrass to grow, let alone tomatoes. It's much easier to keep a bit of calamine and Milk of Magnesia in the cabin.

Hunters and Fishermen can understand why doctors have turned their backs on them and prefer urban practices. That's where the money is. While we can give them credit for their amazing carpentry, replacing hearts and gizzards and atomizing kidney stones without resorting to the knife and all that. Still, some of us wish they'd direct attention to curing the sicknesses more commonly found beyond the borders of big cities. We wish they'd stop fooling around with Thrombocytopenic Pupura and Lupus Erythematosis and spend some time looking for ways to treat the truly ghastly disorders that commonly afflict members of the hunting/fishing fraternity,

They could start by developing an antidote for that alarming and dismaying malady called Grouse Hunter's Twitch. GHT Syndrome is unknown in other populations but common in upland bird hunters. The malady reaches epidemic proportions in late October and early November, but quickly subsides thereafter and enters a dormant state in December.

GHT consists of the sudden and rapid contraction of muscle fibers causing involuntary gasps of surprise and the jumping and revolving in mid-air while dropping a shotgun. Its cause appears to be the explosive whirring sound made by a grouse when it bursts from cover near the hunter's feet.

Personally, I wish the medics would do something about Hexagenaphobia but I'm sure they won't. As far as can be ascertained, I'm the only one who suffers from it and neither doctors nor the pharmaceutical companies will waste their time producing pills to sell to such a limited market.

I can, however, attest to the disease's debilitating effect. I've spent many a sleepless night because of it and, on a few occasions, it has almost kept me from trout fishing. Hexagenaphobia is the fear that real insects will attack me and try to mate with the artificial Green Drake flies I have hand-tied and stuck into the sheepskin band on my fishing hat.

Canis Melancholia, on the other hand is a widespread ailment. It attacks men - old and young alike. Each year I contribute to the Canis Melancolia Research Foundation in the hope they will find a way of treating the overwhelming dejection that occurs when you realize your $500 dog can't hunt worth beans. The dejection is often transformed into panic terror by the fear that your wife will find out about it.

Don't become disheartened, comrades. During the last 100 years the medical profession has moved from grave robbing to laser surgery. Perhaps in the next 100 years they'll tackle important tasks - like the ones listed above.

The Madness of Ulrich

The Homo sapiens, the psychiatrists advise us, displays a widespread disposition toward insanity. I believe they are right. Only insanity can explain mankind's irrational behavior. Marriage, modern popular (so-called) music and the re-election of liberals to Congress can only be explained by the existence of a widespread susceptibility to lunatic derangement. Latent aberrant behavior lies deeply within every one of us. It can burst to the surface at any time and take control of our life.

Ulrich Schmid was considered by his friends and associates to be reasonably rational. He was an accomplished fly fisherman and could use a scatter gun with admirable efficiency. Woodcock were known to come to him waving little white flags of surrender when he entered their part of river bottom land.

Ulrich was regularly employed. He owned a four wheel drive vehicle, a good German Shorthair, a complete collection of necessary hunting and fishing accoutrement and a mute wife. No question about it; Ulrich had it made. He often proclaimed his good fortune was a result of the canons of behavior that ruled his life. He said he did not drink, smoke, gamble or chase women. He did, however, admit to lying a lot.

On any Saturday morning when the weather and the game laws allowed it, Ulrich could be found in some woodsy setting, dirty and unshaven with a shotgun or a fly rod in his hand and smelling faintly of Wild Turkey or cordite.

Today, he is no longer seen on trout streams or in grouse

covert. Canvassbacks fly unmolested over the marshy spot when his artfully camouflaged duck blind once stood. His double barrel rusts from disuse. His graphite rod collects dust. He has abandoned and is abandoned by his former friends. His dog won't speak to him. Today Ulrich is no longer rational. He has lost contact with reason. His mind is diseased. He has gone mad. He has descended into a disgraceful and depraved state. In short, Ulrich has taken up golf.

Man's inclination towards madness is one of the salient characteristics that distinguished him from the lesser beasts. Bunny rabbits do not go mad. The bunny rabbit community maintains no insane asylums. The perceptive reader will remember bunny rabbits do not play golf.

Paranoia and schizophrenia are unknown in the world of Bluebill, Red Head and Green Wing Teal. Those ducks, you will notice, do not hang around caddy shacks. Oh, to be sure, Mallards are sometimes found in water holes. That's because they have a marvelous sense of the ridiculous and are tickled by the antics golfers display around water hazards.

Frankly, comrades, I don't understand why anyone would waste his time committing golf. The concept of the game can be captured in a few minutes by anyone with an intellectual capacity greater than that of a vegetable. The whole idea is: Get the little ball in the hole. Then do it again - and again - and again. The next step consists of repeating the process over and over and over again. Get the little ball in the little hole.

What do golf addicts do in the winter time when the ground is covered with snow and they can't find the little hole? They'll go into debt to get enough cash to go to Florida, live with the cockroaches and alligators and get the little ball in the little hole down there. If they have attained bad credit risk status, the golfers will stay up north and sit transfixed in front of a television set while they watch other people make obscene amounts of money by getting the little ball in the little hole.

Golf is not a game. It is an obsession. It is a madness and golfers are addicts. Golfers start out by telling themselves: "I can stop whenever I want to. I'll just play one hole." Of course, they play one hole - and then another - and then another. Soon they can be found in the early morning, clutching brown paper bags and squatting beside pro shops, waiting for them to be opened. The brown paper bags are meant to keep normal people from knowing tees and golf balls are hidden inside them.

This is what happened to Ulrich. The so-called "game" of golf has dragged him into a disgraceful and humiliating condition. On any Saturday morning, go to the golf place he habituates. You'll have a hard time recognizing him. He is clean shaven. His shoes are shined. He is dressed in pressed slacks and wears a clean shirt with an alligator embroidered on it. It's disgusting. To think a man I so admired could sink so low.

I suppose it can be argued society owes nothing to Ulrich and those who, like him, have abandoned the fields and streams. They point to the positive effects of golf addiction. As the numbers of golfers grow, there will be more room at Ducks Unlimited banquets; fewer trout fishermen will crowd your favorite stretch of the river; fewer idiots will fire at you during deer season.

Some people contend the golfers should be treated like lepers - rounded up and quarantined on some remote Pacific Island. It would be a reasonable way of handling the problem, but I take a different approach. I believe we can stop the rampaging golfing epidemic and reclaim its victims. Our task is daunting. Anti-golf vaccines have proven ineffective. Even our school systems conspire against us. Some of them actually consider golf to be a sport and encourage our children to join their teams and participate in the "game".

There's no point in asking the government to help. Too many Congressmen play golf. (Congressmen are particularly susceptible to idiotic behaviors.) I propose we attack the problem ourselves. I intend to form a group to be called Golfer's Anonymous. If we are advised of any sportsman who begins to show signs of golf addiction, I will visit the poor fellow and beat the hell out of him with a 4 iron. (I think that's the right club.)

Casting for Musky

Author's Note: The following is a true account. At least, it is a reasonably true account. Well - there may have been some embellishments to make the account more readable and I suppose, you should take into consideration the fact that fishermen sometimes (almost always) have great difficulty in distinguishing between what really happened and what might have happened. In addition, sports writers, generally, have a well deserved reputation for dishonesty. Still, it could have happened.

Another Author's Note: You've often heard the phrase: "Only the names have been changed to protect the innocent". In this story, no names have been mentioned in order to protect the guilty. Thus, we are in harmony with the current legal system, the decisions of our learned judges and the finding of the juries of our peers which make sure the guilty are protected and the innocent can go hang

* * * * *

The Muskellunge is called "the fish of a thousand casts". Catching a Musky requires casting, casting - indefatigable casting. A lucky fisherman may boat one after only 999 casts. Others may take more, but casting is central to successful Musky fishing. The neophyte who has not developed the skill may catch nothing more than a bit of hell - and that is what happened last September.

The main character in the tale was sitting in a boat in the middle of a northern lake. His companions watched as he constructed what he called "his secret Musky weapon". He began with two feet of cowbells, usually used for salmon in the Puget Sound. Then he attached a plug the size of a legal walleye. For good measure, he added a good sized Daredevil to a trailing line. The entire contraption was weighted by a sinker which resembled a medium sized platano banana. The whole combination was much heavier than a mature stem of large sized platano bananas.

Our hero's fellow fishermen watched with interest and made various suggestions concerning what he could do with the lure. The suggestions were punctuated with raucous laughter. As he readied for the first cast of his special multi-plugged lure, the men who shared his boat limited themselves to the casting of aspersions. Ignoring them, our hero cocked his throwing arm and gave a mighty heave. The weird device took flight. The weigh of the lure jerked the rod from his hand. Rod, reel and attachments came to rest under more then twenty feet of dark water, never to again enjoy the light of day.

If you are going to throw your rod overboard, take my advice. Don't do it in the presence of witnesses. They are quite apt to make unkind comments. In fact, I guarantee you will be the target of a verbal assault unwitnessed since the liberal press discovered a conservative who unseated a liberal Senator. For example

"Without exception, everyone who has fished with you has claimed you are an incompetent fisherman. You've just proven them wrong. That was an excellent cast. The rod flew well over fifty feet before it hit the water.

"I believe the North American record for heaving a rod over the side is forty two feet. Let's measure your effort. You may have a chance to be included in the next issue of the Guinness Book of Records. I intend to nominate you."

- or -

"On the whole your technique is acceptable, but you made one serious mistake. You let go of the rod. Had you retained your grip, the weight of that Mickey Mouse lure would have jerked you overboard, too. Then we could have had a good laugh as we started the motor, pulled away and watched you try to swim to shore. I'd bet five dollars you'd have made it, but - frankly - I wouldn't have been the least bit disappointed if I lost."

- or -

"Don't pay any attention to us. Ignore us. You'll only have to put up with our shameless insolence for another 6 days. After all, we'll only be able to pick on you for 18 hours a day. We'll sleep for 6 hours and then you can get some rest - presuming your conscience will allow you to rest after your miserable and clumsy display."

-or-

"I'm sure there's a slight possibility we'll forget about it when we get back to town, but, on the other hand, it may be best if you prepared yourself to hear the incident broadcast to your few remaining friends, your close and distant relatives and to strangers in the far reaches of the county. It might even appear in the newspapers."

- or -

"Look on the brighter side. The rod was worth maybe a hundred and ten dollars and the line and reel, perhaps, another seventy five. Add another fifty dollars for all that hardware and - let's see - lead goes for about eighty cents a pound - add another eight dollars for that sinker.

"You only lost two hundred and forty three dollars as a result of that one magnificent cast. You'll probably claim three times that amount as an uncompensated casualty loss in you Income Tax Returns and get it all back from the government. Hmmmm. I wonder if they still pay bounties for turning in Income Tax cheats."

- or -

"I hope you won't take this personally. I mean it as a constructive criticism. Your cursing and your swearing comes as a surprise to me. Endlessly repeating a reference to the male offspring of a lady canine - the only change being the place-ment of the emphasis - brings no credit to you. Unless you change your errant ways, you will never again be invited to join us on a fishing expedition.

"You have developed a certain attractive rhythm to your swearing, but you'll have to expand your vocabulary and use some imagination if you wish to attain expert status. I recommend you sign up for a course in the Art of Cursing at the Technical Institute. In the meantime, you'll be on probation until you show proficiency in the matter. You know what probation means: carrying the wood, tending the fire and washing the dishes."

* * * * *

That Income Tax suggestion is a good one. I can recover a goodly part of my loss from the IRS. I may be able to disguise my involvement a bit and sell the story to some magazine. If it's published, I'll end up making a nice profit.

Eternal Life

I suspect I am not going to go to heaven. I know this statement will come as a shock to all of you and many will be prompted to quickly and vehemently argue with me. I admit you will be able to come forward with what the judges call "clear and convincing proof" that I am wrong. Still, my opinion will not change.

Let me explain. Except for feeling excruciating pain whenever I hear a saxophone, I am ignorant in matters musical - and this includes the harp. I am tone deaf. My attempts at singing have made competent musicians grimace. Tears ran down the cheeks of others.

Were I to be allowed in heaven, I could not play the harp nor sing in the heavenly choir without profoundly disrupting the perfect harmony of the place. In addition, I suspect some of the angels might object to my cigars.

This would, I fear, tempt many of those in the angelic choir (as well as many of those who were within hearing range) to resort to language not usually associated with the Cherubim. It would certainly cause them to petition higher authority for my removal from the Elysian Fields.

No, friends, they'll never let me in up there.

On the other hand, the people who know about such things assure me I won't go the Hell. This came as an acute disappointment to me because I had looked forward to meeting so many of you during my afterlife.

Because I am an attorney, the devil has barred me from

Hades. He claims there are already too many lawyers down there. He says they are a disagreeable lot, spending all their time questioning his jurisdiction, disputing his authority, and generally raising hell. He'll have no more of them.

It looks like I'm going to live forever.

The Honest Angler

Our sixteenth president was called "Honest Abe". After extensive research, historians have been unable to produce a single record showing Abraham Lincoln had ever been a fisherman. This does not mean to say all fishermen are liars. On the contrary, statistics show every state in the Union (with the possible exception of Arkansas) contains a few fishermen who are occasionally accused of being truthful.

Personally, I doubt such a charge could be proven in a court of law. After all, even the most honorable of us, if put under extreme pressure, can resort to stating an untruth. Such overwhelming pressure might be represented by questions like: Where did you catch that big Speckled Trout?", or, "What time is it?" Still, a few of us have been able to resist the temptations leading lesser men to lie.

In order to give appropriate public recognition to those paragons of virtue, the Society for the Encouragement of Trout Fishing and Low Tariffs on Imported Wines has created the prestigious and coveted Honest Angler Award. The Honest Angler designation is valued not only because it is an honor conferred by one's own fishing peers, but also because it can produce substantial financial reward. In 2007, Mitchell Stoychoff, received a handsome fee when the TV program, Unexplained Mysteries, devoted an entire program to his receipt of the Award.

Jerry Koenig is one of the many who have sought the honor. He has genuinely attempted to meet the strict conditions required of those who would be considered for the prize and he came very close to achieving his goal. Last February, the SFTEOTFALTOIW (the acronym by which the Society is designated) held its annual Awards and Cabin Fever Prevention Banquet at The 400 Bar, Grill and Live Bait Shop.

Jerry had been nominated and was considered to have the inside track, although some favored a fisherman who also claimed he had told no lies during the prior year. His proof consisted of a letter from the warden showing he had spent the entire time in solitary confinement at the State Prison. At the last moment, that nominee produced a surprise affidavit attacking the credibility of Jerry Koenig. The affidavit concerned itself with events on the opening day of that year's trout season. It said:

"A friend and I were fishing on what appeared to be an excellent stretch of water on the South Branch of the Oconto River. At 8:00 a.m. we came upon a fisherman I now know to be Mr. Jerry Koenig.

"As we approached him, he pulled a small .380 Automatic from beneath his waders and, in rapid succession, fired four shots into the water near the shore line. Having thus succeeded in securing our attentions, Koenig explained that he had shot at a rattlesnake.

"He told us lots of rattlers nested in the rocks near the banks of that part of the river and, having been roused from their hibernations by the warmer May temperature, the short tempered and evil reptiles had left their dens and entered the water in search of frogs, muskrats and other meat.

"This, Koenig volunteered, represented no danger to the fisherman if he was armed and didn't allow the snakes to get any closer than six feet from you. He said the snakes made fishing that short part of the South Branch difficult, but what the hell, who's afraid of aggressive, particularly vicious and extremely poisonous snakes? It adds spice to the fishing - a dimension not enjoyed by those who fish a quarter of a mile above or below here.

"My friend and I thought it might be prudent to by-pass that part of the river, and we did."

After a full discussion of the contents of the affidavit, eight of the fifteen members of the Awards Committee refused to believe Jerry's own admission that he hadn't lied during the year. He was not given the Honest Angler Award. He did receive the Closest to Being Honest Award at the banquet. It wasn't enough. Jerry was devastated. Moreover, he was forever foreclosed from securing the Honest Angler Award unless he promised to discontinue his humanitarian practice of warning fellow fishermen of imminent danger from non-existent venomous snakes.

Jerry faced a terrible dilemma. He wanted the Award, but that part of the South Branch was his favorite fishing spot and the aforementioned ploy had consistently discouraged others from encroaching on his domain. The price of the Honest Angler Award became the loss of his exclusive use of some of the finest water in the state.

This spring, Jerry changed his tactics. On opening day, he hid his fishing paraphernalia behind a stump and walked up to the stream dressed in clean, neatly pressed khakis, carrying a handful of official looking Notices. He did not say he was a Game Warden. He did not say the badge prominently displayed on his Smokey-the-Bear hat really showed he was a member of the town's Volunteer Fire Department.

Jerry never said the Notices he posted on trees were, in fact, new and complicated DNR rules announcing impossible to understand Catch and Release regulations as well as possession limitations that depended upon size, species, gender, weight and time of day of the catch.

He did, however, tell everyone who came past to be aware of the DNR fishing regulations and he did say DNR rules would be strictly enforced. Then he sat on a log where he had an unrestricted view of the entire stretch of water. It didn't take long before he had the place to himself AND HE HADN'T TOLD A SINGLE LIE.

If that deaf, mute fisherman doesn't get nominated this year, I think Jerry has a good chance to receive the Award.

State v. Scheinert

The rights of outdoorsmen have been determined by opinions of the Supreme Courts of the various States. It behooves all who are interested in hunting and fishing to become acquainted with these landmark statements of the law. Such a decision was made in the matter of the State of Wisconsin v. Scheinert.

In the 1920's a very successful vaudeville act was called "Pete Scheinert and His Friend Oakie". Pete and Oakie were, indeed, close friends. Pete was the straight man and Oakie was his trained bear. After the stock market crashed in 1929, things went to hell in the vaudeville business. Theaters closed or were converted into movie houses. Hard times fell upon Pete and Oakie.

By 1933, their only income was earned from participation in Shriner's parades. They faced starvation. Pete gave serious consideration to eating Oakie. The situation was equally bad for the bear and Oakie gave serious consideration to eating Pete. Discussions between the two of them were not productive. They were unable to reach any agreement on who was to eat who and it seems as if the act would break up. Their economic and culinary problems were, however, resolved to their mutual satisfaction.

You will remember the early 1930's exploits of Baby Face Nelson, Machine Gun Kelly, John Dillinger, Bonnie and Clyde and Ma Barker's gang. They all received wide publicity in the national press. However the rash of bank robberies in rural northern Wisconsin went largely unreported and you may not have heard about them.

In late 1933, a hysterical bank clerk in Gresham told the Shawano County Sheriff how a large man dressed in a black fur coat entered the bank carrying a shotgun, a paper bag and a note demanding she clean out the till, put the money in the bag and give it to the robber. After receiving the money, the robber picked up a waste basket, balanced it on his nose and, acknowledging the applause of the bank's customers, backed out the door. Then he quickly ran off through the woods.

The bank clerk was unable to give a further description of the robber since he wore a ski mask and, excepting for a few grunts and growls, hadn't spoken a word. The police were baffled. Shortly thereafter, the bank in Argonne was robbed. The same modus operandi was reported. Every few months thereafter, a northern Wisconsin bank was robbed by what became known as "the Fur Coated Bandit".

Surprisingly, finger prints were never found in spite of reports that the Fur Coated Bandit never wore gloves. It was noted, however, the robber had a lot of hair on his hands, his fingernails were quite dirty and he needed a manicure. Equally surprising was the lack of footprints. The escape routes through the woods were specifically pointed out, but neither the Sheriff nor the investigators from the State Crime Lab were able to find any footprints.

Evidences of the presence of bears were noticed. The Wisconsin Conservation Commission - seeing reports of bear spoor and bear tracks at the sites of the various robberies - concluded a bear population explosion was under way. The Commissioners immediately took action. They opened a special bear hunting season in northern Wisconsin.

In a forest adjacent to Armstrong Creek, a hunter saw movement in the brush and fired. When he went to see what he shot at, he found he had grazed the head of a man in a ski mask wearing a black fur coat. The wounded man was unconscious. The marksman believed he had shot another bear hunter and brought him to the nearest hospital. When the nurse tried to take his coat off, the man objected. He became surly and snapped at her. Then the telling discovery was made. The wounded "man" was a black bear.

Suspicions being thus aroused, the Sheriff's Department was notified and a search of the area of the shooting incident was undertaken. A shotgun, a paper bag and a robbery note addressed to the Armstrong Creek Bank were discovered. The District Attorney of Marinette County dismissed the charge of Reckless Use of a Firearm, which had been brought against the hunter, The DA was convinced that he had captured the Fur Coated Bandit.

Problems arose immediately. The bear refused to talk. Repeated grilling of the animal elicited only a few grunts. Oakie wasn't about to implicate his good friend, Pete. The paper bag could not be traced, but the shotgun was a different matter. Serial numbers showed it had been purchased from a Milwaukee pawn shop in 1933 by one Peter Scheinert.

Believing that name was an alias used by the bear, the police brought the pawn shop owner to Marinette. The bear, a few politicians and other unsavory local characters were put into a police line-up. The pawn shop owner was unable to identify the bear as the one who bought the shotgun from his shop. He insisted the purchaser of the shotgun was clean shaven and had shorter ears. Nevertheless, the D.A. brought charges against the bear, but was unable to secure a conviction.

All criminal statutes say it is "against the law for a person to..." etc., etc. Oakie's attorney convinced the Judge his client was not a "person" and had the State's case against the bear thrown out of Court. Thus, an important principle, famous in conservation circles, was established: A bear cannot be charged with bank robbery.

An even more important decision was forthcoming.

During their investigation, the Sheriff learned a man named Peter Scheinert was living near Woodruff in a place called Little Bohemia. The bank robbery charge was never brought against him because he has solid alibis placing him far from the banks when they were robbed.

The Crime Lab, however, found traces of bank carpeting on the bear's feet and traces of the same carpeting on the clutch, brake and gas pedal of Pete's car. That fact plus the proof that Pete had bought the shotgun was enough to charge him with being an accessory, before, during and after a felony.

The Judge, however, immediately dismissed the State's case. His decision was appealed and, in upholding the lower Court ruling, the Supreme Court of the State of Wisconsin established one of the great conservation law precedents. In freeing Pete, the Court cited the Second Amendment to the Constitution of the United States which guarantees the right of all citizens to keep and arm bears.

Matching the Hatch

The successful modern day trout fly fisherman is half delicate fly line manipulator, half con artist and half stream biologist. He is much more imaginative than, say, a mathematician or an accountant who believe two halves are enough.

A good fisherman must be able to "read" a stream to determine a trout's likely feeding station. A good fisherman must be able to drop his line at a spot where the fly will float over that feeding station in a natural and convincing manner. The object is to convince the trout it is a real insect. In addition, a good trout fisherman must be able to tie a fly with such deception, guile and trickery that a trout will think a metal hook covered with hair and feathers is a living and edible insect.

The presence of these three abilities, all by themselves, will not produce a successful fly fisherman. One element is still missing. That element is the ability to correctly identify the hatch coming off the water and select an artificial fly of the same type, size, shape and color of those flying insects. In other words, the ability to match the hatch which represents the food the trout are then eating.

A PhD. in entomology (or bugology, as it is technically known) is not necessary to be able to match the hatch. Most trout fishermen know when to fish with an Elk Hair Caddis, but they wouldn't know a Hesperophylax if it knocked them down and sat on them. (The possibility of that happening is remote. The Hesperophylax is a very small caddis. Still, when one is out there in the wild woods, one can't be too careful.)

Many of the entomologists and academicians who are expert in Bugology spend their time fooling around in university zoology laboratories. They get government grants and, I suppose, it might be argued they do some good work. The real advances in the science of matching the hatch, however, come from laymen who spend their time outdoors on trout streams.

Even attorneys, Editors of outdoor magazines, DNR commissioners and other uneducated people are capable of matching the hatches rising from trout streams. They develop the ability through careful observation and experimentation. And therein lies the tale.

Few trout fishermen will wade the streams after dark. They prefer to spend the evening hours in a cabin, sipping and lying to their associates about their successes during the day. I count myself among that group.

Other fly fishermen will go after trout when the sun has set. As far as I'm concerned, part of the joy of fly fishing is being able to see the alder brush that snags your fly on your back cast. At night you are constantly being hung up in shrubbery you didn't even know was there. It takes all the fun out of it.

Nelson Hartley was, exclusively, a daylight trout fisherman. Two years ago he was wading in a trout stream long after the sun had set. He wasn't experimenting with a nighttime fishing. He was lost. He knew if he walked down stream long enough he'd come to a bridge or a cabin. With only faint light from the moon and the stars, he followed the current. It was then he noticed for the very first time a peculiar hatch flying above and around him.

Nothing in his fly box came close to a match. He suspected he was looking at a hitherto unknown fly, unique in the world of the trout fisherman. As he stumbled down the stream (and, occasionally, beneath its surface), he watched the strange hatch. Then a flash of inspiration hit him and he saw exposed before him the prospects for a brighter trout fishing future

Nelson felt (a) if he could produce a new artificial fly which would match that midnight hatch, and (b) if the fly were so artful devised it would con the trout into trying to eat it, and (c) if he could patent the pattern and find a company which would manufacture and market it, and (d) if he could negotiate a reasonable royalty agreement with that company, then (e) he would make a mint and be able to retire and fish for the rest of his life.

To further his plan, Nelson's first step was to review all of the bug books he had collected over the years. He could find no written reports describing the large insect he had seen. His suspicions of the unique quality of his discovered hatch was confirmed. His next step was to study the hatch in the field and learn all of its characteristics. Armed with that knowledge, he would proceed to tie the artificial fly which would make him wealthy.

The results of Nelson's investigations were somewhat equivocal, but much was learned. The hatch begins in the springtime and extends throughout the summer and well into the early autumn months. Due to Nelson's own extreme near sightedness and the lack of light available during his nighttime observations, his reports on the emerging nymphs were somewhat sketchy. He concluded the emerging nymph was so tiny it could not be seen. At least he never saw a single one of them breaking the surface of the stream.

According to Nelson, once the bug left its nymph stage, the insect enjoys explosive growth. In seconds it metamorphosised into the adult stage and a body length of perhaps two inches is attained. The adult has large membranous wings. It is brown or black in color and its flight is erratic.

Nelson's hatch has other unique characteristics. The insect has only two legs instead of the usual six. It is not invertebrate and does not have an exoskeleton or the common three segmented body. It does, however, have two large protuberances, like ears, extending from its head, and it has teeth. While some insects leave the water and spend time hanging on the bottom sides of leaves, Nelson's hatch spends the daylight hours clinging upside down in caves or church belfries or other dark places.

Nelson is now tying a fly which, he assures me, will match the insect. Look for it soon in all well supplied fly shops. It will be called Nelson's Vampire

Dog Talk

There are people who think dogs can't talk. These are the kind of folks who are natural born skeptics, the ones who don't own dogs, the abjectly ignorant and the ones who are out looking for a fist fight.

If you give a dog trainer enough of his favorite alcoholic beverage, he'll admit he has learned how to train dogs by listening to their conversation as they rest in their kennels after a hard day in the field. It may cost you three or four dollars for a gallon of their preferred kind of Dago Red, but the investment is worth it. Try some of it yourself. It will open your eyes. It may also make you cough.

Most dogs don't speak clearly and, admittedly, some are difficult to understand. Nevertheless, to claim that dogs don't talk is like claiming Finlanders or Burmese or people from Arkansas don't talk, merely because they speak a foreign language that is strange and almost impossible to comprehend.

Owners of English Setters face no such problem. They will admit their dogs speak grammatically correct English, but with a clipped accent. A Pekinese, on the other hand, speaks a very obscure Chinese dialect. The Poodles prefer French and Spaniels incline toward the Spanish, but all dogs can learn to express themselves in English.

Charlie Ainsworth once owned an Irish Setter. It spoke English. Whenever the dog felt like it, it barked it fluently. If Charlie asked it: "What was the name Jackie Gleason used in the Honeymooners?" the dog, with his quaint Irish accent, would answer; "Ralph, Ralph". If Charlie inquired: "Where is the chimney?" the dog would always respond: "Roof, roof". Charlie's dog was a very intelligent animal.

Charlie sold the Setter to a hardwoods lumber mill. The dog was perfectly suited for its new employment. It would jump into the mill pond where the hardwood logs were floating and identify the logs by the smell of its outer layer. The dog, you see, was an expert on barks.

Bob Moore had a hunting dog named "Doc". Being an English Setter, it didn't have the problem of the Weimaraners, the Vislas or the German Shorthairs. It didn't have to learn a second language. It was a big, smart English speaking dog.

I think it was Doc's very intelligence that destroyed not only its ability as a hunting dog, but also its relationship with Bob. I'd usually hunt with Bob two or three times a season. We'd give Doc a workout in pheasant country and shoot at the birds he'd find for us. Bob claimed Doc was extraordinarily talkative, but I never actually heard it talk. The dog always seemed so engrossed in the business of sniffing out and pointing birds that it didn't have time to engage me in casual conversation.

I didn't get a chance to hunt with Bob for a few seasons. We finally got together last September. Bob was training a young Brittany and Doc was nowhere to be seen. Of course, I remembered Doc as an excellent hunter and Bob told me it had become an even more proficient bird dog. When I inquired about the animal, Bob told me what had happened.

One day Doc came to Bob and asked for a name change. After the dog explained the reason for its request, Bob could see his point. The dog was getting tired of bumping into rabbits who'd ask it: "What's up, Doc?" and then smirk and giggle. It was demeaning.

Bob gave Doc a new name. It was a more respectable name

and added to the animal's stature (but with no concomitant increase in pay). Thenceforth, "Doc" was called "Doctor". The dog was satisfied for a while, but then the animal began to change for the worse. He was developing an overactive ego.

Doctor's new name went to the dog's head. It was so impressed by the title of "Doctor" that it felt it he was better than the other dogs with names like "Spike" or "Spot" or "Pepper". Its ego blossomed as did the dog's feelings of superiority. It began to feel it was Bob's social and intellectual equal.

It didn't take long before Doctor became quite temperamental and independent. One evening it approached Bob and insisted it be given new name. It wanted to be called "Physician". Reluctantly, Bob agreed to the animal's demands.

Physician became increasingly uncontrollable and the relationship between Bob and the dog rapidly deteriorated. Physician forgot who was the master and who was the dog. It paid no attention to hand signals. It disregarded spoken commands. It wouldn't respond to the whistle. It ranged outside of shotgun range. It hunted when and where it wanted. It actually got testy with hunters who missed shots.

Bob tried desperately to reform the animal. He even sent it back to dog training school. Nothing seemed to work. Physician just got worse and worse. The trainer claimed the dog was incorrigible and was teaching the other animals to become so independent it was impossible to train any of them. Finally, Physician stopped attending classes and was thrown out of the school in disgrace. Bob did his best to rehabilitate the animal, but without effect.

The relationship between man and beast finally ruptured on an afternoon in mid-October. Bob and Physician were hunting pheasants. Bob intended to enter an adjacent section of standing corn, but the dog wanted to hunt in a field of stubble.

It wouldn't have been so bad if the two had calmly discussed their differences and settled them in a reasonable manner, but the dog insisted on having its own way. It went too far when it started walking to the stubble field and ordered Bob to "Heel". That was the straw that broke the camel's back.

Bob abandoned the dog on the spot. He turned and stormed off in another direction. The last contact Bob had with the English Setter was when he shouted back at the animal: "Physician, heel thyself."

The Malthusian Theory

Back in the 1790's, Richard Malthus took a close look at the human race and observed its number was increasing at a geometric and not an arithmetic progression. He became excited by his discovery, then nervous and, finally, filled with foreboding. An exploding population, he posited, would eat us all out of house and home. According to Richard's calculations, only war, famine and epidemic disease could control the number of people on earth.

In this enlightened twenty-first century, though overpopulation seriously threatens the earth, the promoting of natural catastrophes is a pretty tough occupation. Anyone who has the temerity to suggest them as a device to solve overpopulation problems can expect to receive stern reprimands from both the liberal and the conservative media. He will be roundly damned by believers, agnostics and atheists, alike.

No civilized person would consider suggesting the restraint of population growth through war, famine or pestilence. And yet...?

While I'm not particularly infatuated by their socialist tendencies, ants have some good qualities. They work hard. They're temperate. They don't play golf. In spite of what their colonies do to your lawn, you are probably not unalterably opposed to their continued existence. Nevertheless, if you happen to have a cabin being eaten by an exploded population of Carpenter ants, believe me, eradication by war, famine and pestilence will all be thoroughly investigated.

Famine is not the best method of eradicating Carpenter ants. By the time their presence is noted, they will have already eaten 39% of your cabin. They could live for years on the remaining 61%. By that time, as Richard Malthus theorized, you will have been eaten out of house and home. Starving them by removing the source of their food could be accomplished by the Draconian measure of burning down your cabin. I would suggest it only as the last resort.

Pestilence is an interesting alternative. In the 1300's, the Plague, a/k/a Black Death, was successful in killing off three quarters of the population of Europe and Asia in about twenty years. The problem is: How do you infect Carpenter ants with a loathsome and fatal illness? How can you train infected fleas to bite rats and rats to bite Carpenter ants without getting bit yourself? Even if you successfully overcome that problem, the Carpenter ants may get hold of some streptomycin and survive the disease.

The answer is chlordane. It will kill Carpenter ants dead, dead, dead. Unfortunately, its use may have an unintended consequence. It might kill you, too - but desperate conditions call for desperate measures.

None of us will get hysterical when we see a mouse. We rather enjoy them. They don't eat much. They don't steal a lot of stuffing from the mattress when they build their nests. Only occasionally do they turn the white flour into buckwheat flour. In that case, it's you own fault for not storing the flour in a closed metal coffee can.

A mouse, two mice, three mice (blind or otherwise), even four mice are no cause for alarm. However, population explosions are apt to occur. A few years ago, I didn't have a single mouse in my cabin. They were all married and had large families. When mice have a baby boom, they start eating the cabin and that is unacceptable behavior. Holes appear at the bottom of the front door, around the baseboard and where the ceiling meets the walls.

At night, emboldened by their large numbers, mice no longer pussyfoot around. (That's a mixed metaphor if I ever saw one). They chew and rasp and gnaw and munch and crunch and nibble at various parts of your building and sleep is impossible because of their confounded racket. They'll shut up if you swear at them or throw a boot against the wall, but only until you've begun to doze off. Then they reconvene, set up their tiny cross-cut saws and start in again with a vengeance.

I don't like to poison mice, even when they so richly deserve it. Other creatures eat their carcasses and innocent animal bystanders get hurt. However, when pressed beyond the limit of human endurance, I will do whatever is necessary.

I contacted the Power and Light Company. They seem to have a problem disposing of their atoms once they've been used at the power plant. I thought I might be able to pick up a carton or two, cheap. I planned to wrap the isotopes in cheese. The mice would eat the cheese, go back to their nests and irradiate the whole wretched clan.

The Power and Light people wouldn't cooperate with me. That's monopoly for you - to hell with the public. Perhaps it's just as well. I dreamed of meeting a mutant atomic mouse behind the sauna building. It was two feet tall, had lots of sharp teeth, long claws and it glowed in the dark.

Natural warfare took care of the problem. A family of weasels moved in and cleaned out the mouse population in a hurry. I've never been exceptionally enthusiastic about weasels. They share the irascible dispositions and ill-tempered grouchiness of the fisher, the wolverine and the rest of their cousins, but they sure did a job on those mice.

When they moved on without doing damage to the cabin, I began to harbor kind thoughts about the bloodthirsty little beggars. The mice had been terminally discouraged, the weasels had moved on and the cabin was no longer endangered. Or, so I thought.

Then the unmistakable sign of porcupine began to appear. They were chewing on the 4 by 8 plywood sheets forming the outside walls of my cabin buildings. They were after the glue. I guess it tastes good to porcupines. I had to place a block of salt near the outhouse to keep them from chewing through the door. I gently shoo them away when I find them on the back steps. No other more drastic action has been planned.

You see, I've learned that the Malthusian Theory is irrefutable. Population growth is geometrical and not arithmetical. From ants to mice to porcupines is certainly a geometric progression in size. I treat the porcupines kindly because, if I kill them off, I have no idea of what will next try to destroy my cabin. If the geometric progression continues, I know whatever next attacks my cabin will be big - very big. It might be a black bear. I'm leaving well enough alone.

The Hog Pen

In the winter after the end of the war, Freddie Walman got discharged from the army and I got out of the navy. During our service we never shot at anyone and we didn't have the pleasure of being shot at. We enjoyed our military experience to such an extent that Freddie never bought a brown suit and I never bought a blue one. We got back home as quickly as we could and renewed a friendship that began in grade school.

We both were raised in hunting/fishing families and spent a good deal of our youthful energies in outdoor type pursuits. By the time we had gotten over the shock of returning to civilian life - that is, found a job and got organized - it was springtime and Freddie decided we should build a shack on the eighty acres his family owned up north in good deer country.

On Thursday evening, we'd load the pick-up with the building materials we had scrounged or been forced to buy. On Friday, as soon as we got out of work, we'd leave directly from the plant and drive seventy miles to our building site. We were young and tough. Army surplus sleeping bags, mosquito netting, a gas lantern and some bottle beer provided all the creature comforts we required. Bread and butter and ham and eggs and hamburger and soup kept our bodies and souls together.

We had to cross three forties of government land to get to the Walman property. It was so far back in the woods we felt it was safe to leave the levels and squares, the saws and the hammers, the nails and the shovel under a tarpaulin covered with brush. There were just as many thieves around then, but they were less enterprising or too lazy to go down a mile of bad road just to steal a few tool and some second hand lumber.

Freddie and I were capable of figuring our which side of the handsaw did the cutting, but no one ever accused us of being professional carpenters - or even rank amateurs for that matter. We couldn't afford to hire anyone. We made an agreement. If anyone didn't like the quality of our work, he could stay outside and sleep with the porcupines.

Our investment in lumber was minimal. At night, we'd cruise the town and look for buildings being torn down. That's where our doors and windows and boards came from. Sometimes we'd get the materials after midnight on the assumption the contractor would not want us to bother him with silly questions or get in his men's way when they were working during daylight hours.

Some 2 x 8s from a building demolished when the bank relocated and a couple of old telephone poles composed the first trailer load we hauled up north. When we got back into town late on Sunday evening, we were both convinced the shovel, the post hole digger and the pick were instruments of torture invented by Torquemada during the Spanish Inquisition, but the posts were in the ground and the 2 x 8 joists were within screaming distance of being level. They were spiked together and ready to receive the floor.

By the time the week-end of the opening of the deer season rolled around, almost three walls had been finished, the roof was on and a pot bellied stove (with a flat top for cooking) had been installed in the center of the room.

Al Heins worked at the paper mill. He was invited to hunt with us because he was a hunter, he seemed to be a good guy and he was not allergic to hard work. In addition, he had access to big sheets of used paper mill felt. We needed a good size piece of it to nail across the open side of the building. You could throw a cat through some of the holes in the as yet unfinished floor. Felt could cover those open walls and also act as a kind of rug to keep the wind from blowing under the cabin, up through those cracks and freezing the water in the milk can.

Al got the felt. It was loaded into the trailer with the rest of our deer hunting supplies and paraphernalia. We left for camp as soon as the factory's five o'clock whistle blew. When we got there, Al took one look at our semi-cabin and told us he had seen better hog pens. From that moment on, our deer camp had a name.

That first hunting season was a tough one. We managed to get the felt nailed over the missing fourth wall, but the mercury disappeared into the thermometer's bulb. As the temperature dropped, the wind began to blow. The felt did a lot of back and forth flapping and it was as cold as an ex-girl friend's kiss. There was no aged hardwood for the stove. The cabin heating supply consisted of popple growing in the woods only two months earlier. We took turns feeding the fire.

Our three army cots formed a triangle around that old pot bellied stove. We'd get as close as we could without getting roasted. Still, the side away from the stove nearly froze. We spent the night turning - every hour and in unison - in order to warm up the part of our bodies that had been away from the heat.

There was just enough of a flat surface on the top of the stove to accommodate two containers - a coffee pot and a skillet for ham and eggs in the morning - a soup kettle and a one quart sauce pan for boiling hot dogs in the evening. We had cold cuts for lunch. (Somehow those words don't convey the right image. "Frozen cuts" is a better term.)

The soup was served in the army fashion - once scoop from

the bottom and one scoop from the top. The soup had been badly burned. When we ladled it out we had to be careful not to break loose any of the layer of black stuff coating the bottom of the pan.

Each hot dog was wrapped in a piece of bread and held for a minute or so before eating. It wasn't a religious ceremony. It was a method for warming both the bread and the hand that held it. The other hand was cold. It held a bottle of frigid beer. That's all we had to drink. There wasn't enough room on top of the stove to heat soup, boil hot dogs and percolate coffee.

Al and Freddie and I had a great time. That was a long time ago and I can look back and remember everything we said and did. (I've been accused of remembering things we didn't say or do.) I don't remember if we filled up that year. We didn't keep written records then. I think Al took home a real trophy. Yes, he did.

The next summer Pete Scheinert joined the crew. We had four sets of hands to make the cabin wind proof and, because I never learned the game, they could play three handed Schafskopf. Comparatively speaking, that second deer season was one of sybaritic comfort. The Hog Pen was reasonably warm. We had built some bunk beds and even added two windows for better daytime lighting.

Over the years, the Hog Pen became respectable. The old stove was retired to the Walman barn and replaced by a bottled gas space heater and a real cook stove that contained an oven. We drove a well point and found water at 42 feet. A kitchen area was added to the cabin. The place was insulated. As the crew members increased - there were eight regulars when Al died - the Hog Pen got even bigger. Two separate bunk rooms gave it some real class.

The biggest change came when the electric company wanted to run its lines across a corner of the back forty.

Freddie didn't want to have anything to do with them. Freddie is a reasonable man. He threatened to shoot them if they set a foot on his property. When they offered to run an electric line to the Hog Pen - at no charge - Freddie reluctantly agreed, adding a condition. They had to plant clover over the easement right of way. (Freddie was also a Ruffed Grouse hunter.)

The additions of electric lights, electric blankets, an electric stove and an electric pump got the wives interested in the Hog Pen. It didn't take long before the place was paneled, had a real rug on the floor, pictures on the walls, curtains over the windows and a television set. By that time the second generation was using the place and all sorts of amenities began to appear. The young guys did most of the heavy work and we old-timers would sit back, direct traffic and tell them how tough it used to be in the old days.

Well, times change, I guess. The old gang fell apart. Lem and Karl and Pauly have joined Al. Jack writes from Arizona every November. He moved there after his by-passes. The youngsters bought the Hog Pen from Freddie. They changed its name to The Deerslayer's Inn and formed a corporation. I don't want to go back there. Not even in the summer time. It's just not the same.

Last week I got a call from Freddie. He bought five acres up in Forest County. He got hold of two telephone poles and resurrected the pot bellied stove from the family barn. He wants Pete and me to help him put up a cabin. He's going to call it the Hog Pen. I sure hope we can get the roof on and all four walls up before the deer season starts.

Other Books by Galen Winter

500 WILD GAME AND FISH RECIPES (Editor)

LEGENDARY NORTHWOODS ANIMALS
A Farcical Field Guide

BACKLASH
A Compendium of Lore and Lies (Mostly Lies)
Concerning Hunting, Fishing and the Out-Of-Doors

THE AEGIS CONSIPRACY

THE BEST OF THE MAJOR

THE CHRONICLES OF MAJOR PEABODY

THE JOURNALS OF MAJOR PEABODY

www.ingramcontent.com/pod-product-compliance
Lightning Source LLC
Chambersburg PA
CBHW022024090426
42739CB00006BA/278